WHAT

I

GAINED

THROUGH

MY PAIN

Triumphs After the Trials

By: Nakisha S. James

Mrs. Nakisha S. James

Ordering Information:
For details, contact www.confidentmellc.com.

Print ISBN: 9781661411787

Cover created by: creativepro_81
Publishing/Editing by: ConfidentMe, LLC

Printed in the United States of America on SFI Certified paper.

First Edition

Mrs. Nakisha S. James

INTRODUCTION

First let me start off by saying that this is not one of those drama filled, woe is me, pity party type of books. Nope not this one! What you have in your hands is a collection of real-life experiences that were lived by.... well....ME! God has carried me through a lot over these last 40+ years of my life. And 40 years is a young age, but it can be a long time to go through STUFF! Sometimes I just sit back, and I think how I even made it through everything. Then I remember....God was carrying me. My feet never touched the ground! From growing up with drugs and abuse in the home, pregnancies and abortions, losing my mom at age 15, getting married......getting divorced, single momma hustling, and then moving across the country with nothing but my daughters and our clothes......ALL THIS....and I am still standing! None of this was easy but every bit of it was worth it. It has made me the woman who I am today. I hope sharing my story and my struggles will help those who turn the pages of this book "Gain Through MY Pain" as well. If I can survive this then so can you! Are you ready?? Don't stop here...LET'S GO!!!

Mrs. Nakisha S. James

DEDICATIONS

I must give all honor and thanks to my Lord and Savior Jesus Christ. Without HIM I am nothing. Thank you for carrying me through it all and helping me to GROW through what I GO through.

To my mother Brenda Lipscomb-Rayford who watches down on me from heaven. I miss you tremendously! I hope and pray that I have turned out to be the daughter, the mother, the woman that makes you smile and proud. Rest in Paradise Ma.

To my Grannie, Ms. Altheree Lipscomb-Williams. I lost you early in 2016 and it still seems unreal to me. It was like losing my mom all over again. I miss you and love you dearly. I pray that you are smiling down on me from heaven and that I have made you proud. Rest in Paradise.

To my 4 heart beats; Winter, Serenity, Tayvin and Tajir. You are the reason I breathe. You are the reason I smile. You are the reason I am. You are the reason why I exist. I pray that I continue to make you proud and be the mother that you can model after. I love you with every fiber of my being.

Mrs. Nakisha S. James

Finally, to my soul mate, my best friend, my husband, Titus James. I still look at you and can not believe we are married. Twenty plus years after high school who would have seen this one coming. Well God had it all planned, and I am forever grateful to HIM that HE saw fit to bless me with you. I love you beyond words. Thank you for always supporting me and having my back in whatever I do. I love you!

Mrs. Nakisha S. James

Table of Contents

Letter to Reader

Mrs. Nakisha S. James

CHAPTER 1

Growing up in GI

SO, IT BEGINS

Gary, Indiana! The Hoosiers! My birthplace! The place where it all began for me. Back in the day Gary was well known for its thriving steel mills and the Jackson family. You know...Michael and 'em. I call it home. From the candy store Gold Coast on 5th Ave to Screaming Wheels Roller Rink. To Gowdy's fish to Vohr Elementary and Horace Mann High School. Tasty Freeze on 11th Ave and the inscent man, Gary was where I got my foundation. This is where my story begins. I was born on April 6, 1976, the oldest of two children, my parents would eventually have together. My brother came 2 years later in the summer of 1978. From all the baby pictures and from most of the stories that I've heard, I was just a big fat butterball of happiness. I remember spending time over at my Grannie's house over on 4th and Buchanan. We lived right around the corner on 4th and Pierce.

Mrs. Nakisha S. James

We spent a lot of time at my Grannie's. She would be fussing the whole time too! Everybody in the house was a heffa. (That's heifer.... you know...a baby cow) Why...I have no idea. That was just how my Grannie showed us she loved us. My aunt Thelma and her 2 sons, (my two cousins Chris and Mosco) lived there with her. The house was always full! I don't remember a whole lot about my grandfather...my mother's dad. He died later in the year I was born. I do however remember my Grannie's second husband. Grandad Williams. He was a well-known photographer in Gary. I still have baby pics of myself and my brother with his name stamped at the bottom "Williams Studios." So many memories happened over on 4th Ave.

Not too far down the street on 5th Ave is where my aunt Nae-Nae lived. Right across the street from Horace Mann High School in the 1500 apartment building. To get to Nae Nae's from 4th and Pierce you had to walk down 5th Ave and pass Gold Coast. This little corner store was a staple in our community. Two ladies named "Chicken" and "Stella" worked there. The two sweetest ladies you could ever want to meet. They would always give us kids free candy from out the store. This store had all the little things you would run out of at your house. Milk, bread, butter, eggs. My brother and I was in there often with food stamps to get those things. Yes, I said food stamps! We didn't have an EBT card back in the 80's. You had an actual book of paper stamps in the shape of money that you had to tear out and could only use to purchase food. Gold Coast is no longer open. Ms. Chicken and Ms. Stella have both passed on. But the memories I have from there are the most precious and are forever embedded in me.

Mrs. Nakisha S. James

8

Moving on down 5th Ave toward Nae Nae's you then would pass McDonald's on Grant Street. This was the hangout for a lot of the teens at that time in the 1980's. In pass years there have been a few shootings there sad to say, but to this day it is still standing there. I no longer eat fast foods (well maybe Wendy's) but back in that day this place and White Castle was my mom's favorite stop for us to grab some grub!

After you past 5th and Grant, just a block and a half up you would be at my Nae Nae's building. She lived on the top floor apartment 5. Four flights of stairs! Her apartment was huge! So, I thought when I was a child. Up until I was about 12 or 13 my aunt didn't have any children. She did try but suffered with miscarriages. She even had a child that passed after birth. What a strong woman she is! When my brother and I came over we were like her babies. We WERE her babies. She made us homemade cookies and homemade German Chocolate cake. We loved going over there!!! Auntie Nae-Nae cooked all the food for the holidays. She made the best dressing on the planet!! (Where I got my recipe!) She would make homemade dinners rolls and turkey and pies and everything!! It was by the Grace of God I was not overweight as a child! There are so many fond memories I have there. Then it happened! She gave birth to a baby girl. LaShauna Rene James. My little baby cousin. She was my baby doll! So small and so adorable. Everyone was so happy that God had finally blessed my aunt with a healthy baby. All things seemed good in the hood, right? Keep reading...

Mrs. Nakisha S. James

AUNTIE SHIRLEY

Life seemed to be so beautiful. My brother and I had many Aunts and Uncles and cousins both on my mom and my dad side. But there was one Aunt who's home we loved to go over. That was Auntie Shirley's house. She had a huge house in a part of Gary we called Glen Park. Glen Park was where all the "nicer" homes were. She had like 5 bedrooms and 2 or 3 bathrooms. She had a big basement and a big front and side yard. She was married to Uncle Wiley. He was so nice. I loved him. Before he married Auntie Shirley, he had 3 children from his first wife. They were all older than my brother and me. Two daughters and one son. Anytime my mom and dad took us over there we always wanted to spend the night. Everybody had their own room. Usually my brother and our cousin Chucky would stay in Derek's room when we stayed over. That was Uncle Wiley's son. I would usually sleep with one of his daughters. One night when we spent the night and I was in the bed with Uncle Wiley's daughter/my cousin, I remember her hugging me really tight. At first, I didn't think anything of it. We would hug each other all the time so no big deal. Then she grabbed my hand and she put it down her panties. I was maybe 5 or 6 at the time so I wasn't sure what was going on. When I didn't move, she shoved my hand inside her. It was such an awkward feeling. Then she started to move my hand in and out of her. I think she may have been 16 or 17 at this time. This happened for a little while that night before she eventually she fell off to sleep. I don't think I slept at all that night. The next day I didn't say anything to anyone and neither did she. I knew that something wasn't right, but I didn't know how to explain it. We just went on with our day and played like normal cousins.

Mrs. Nakisha S. James

Some time passed and my brother and I went back over to Auntie Shirley's house to play with our cousins as usual. Once again, we spent the night and I slept with the same cousin. The same thing happened again. This went on for a few months. Every time we would spend the night it would happen. I never said anything to anyone. I didn't think anyone would believe me anyway. ***This was one of those things that you just didn't talk about.** I often wonder if I had told someone what would have happened. Would she have gotten in trouble? Would my family be mad at me? Would she be mad at me for telling on her? How would my mom feel about it? How would my Auntie Shirley feel? So many unanswered questions. I miss my Auntie Shirley. Some years later she passed away. Uncle Wiley remarried and is living well. I haven't talked to any of his kids/my cousins in years. I have tried to forget all of this but sometimes it does creep up in my memory. I just deal with it the best way I can. ***It's not always the men in the family that you have to watch around your little girls.**

SCHOOL DAYZ

My brother and I attended Vohr Elementary School which was right behind Horace Mann High. I still remember some of the teachers there like I was just there yesterday. Mrs. Steele taught first grade. Mrs. Stover and the Charm Club. She also taught 4th grade. Coach Wynn was our gym teacher and Mrs. Pugh was our cheerleading coach. This is where my school life began. I made great friends there

Mrs. Nakisha S. James

that are still my good friends today!! Avis Underwood, Kerre Berry, Keisha Daniel, LaWanda McCoy, Terri Boone, just to name a few. I remember going over to Kerre's home a lot. Her house was right down the street from Vohr. It was huge! Her mom and dad were the nicest parents ever! They would always cook the best meals and I had dinner at there home often. She also had 2 little sisters Erica and Shanail. I always thought all 3 of them were the most beautiful girls. As much time as I spent over to Kerre's, I wanted her to spend time at my home too, but there were some reasons why this could not happen.

We lived in a small red brick house with 2 bedrooms and 1 bath. Our home was right smack in the middle of Pierce St. My brother and I shared a room. We didn't have much at my home but whatever we had I wanted to share with my friends. I wasn't embarrassed but very grateful. I would ask my mom often if I could have Kerre and other friends over. The answer would always be no. "Why Ma!?" I would ask. "NO I SAID and don't ask me again!!" This would always be her answer. It crushed me. I didn't want my friends or their families to feel like I was always at their home eating their food and playing with their toys because I didn't have food or toys at my own home. When I did! I just couldn't share them with any of my friends. As a child (and even today as an adult) I was very observant. I quickly realized why I could never have any of my friends over. Often you would see a continuous cloud of smoke drifting through my home. This was daily. Not because our house was on fire but because the use of marijuana. I believe I got high everyday off the contact. So, if any of my friends came over and then went back home with the smell of "weed" in their clothes Oh, there would have been problems! **Kids are young but far from naïve.** Marijuana was not the only drug I was aware of that was prevalent in my childhood home. I remember the use of Cocaine as well. And you don't want the friends of your children going home telling their parents about the white substance on the plate that they saw. That could turn out really bad! So, at the end of the day there were no play dates, sleepovers, or any of that for me. At least not on 4th and Pierce.

LONG DAYS.... LONGER NIGHTS

As if the drugs were not enough, there were some other challenges I faced in my childhood home. In addition to the drugs, there was a lot of abuse that went on as well. Not toward me or my brother but between my parents. My mom and dad were high school sweethearts. They both attended Horace Mann High School back in the 70's. From what I hear they were inseparable! Right after they both graduated from high school they got married. Then at the age of 20 my mom gave birth to me. They were so young so there wasn't really any room for growth or time to really find out who they were as individual people let alone as husband and wife. It was straight Mommy and Daddy mode. Forty plus years later I can still hear their voices arguing in the next room. Even now when I hear someone talking loud outside or in another room, I get nervous. They may even be having a good time, but I still get nervous. I can't even watch any YouTube or internet videos that involve men and women fighting. I'll get all jittery and teary eyed. I remember one night when I was a child, I was asleep in my room and I heard a lot of loud noises and things breaking in the other room. I woke up and my mom came out of the room all bloodied in the face

Mrs. Nakisha S. James

and she grabbed me as a shield. A few minutes later there was a knock on the front door. It was the police and my aunt Nae Nae. I assume my Mom had a chance to call her amid the fight and then Nae Nae called the cops. They took my dad away in handcuffs. I may have been 6 or 7 years old around this time. I was a child when this happened but that is something I will never forget. ***Our past may not dictate our future but it sure does play a major part.** We went and stayed at my aunt's house that night. The next morning, I remember my mom getting up, getting dressed, and with a busted lip and a black eye she went to work at Gainer Bank on Broadway. She was a bank teller there. She didn't have a job that she could hide behind a computer at a desk or a cubical like many of us have today. She had to face her customers as a bank teller all bruised and battered. What a strong mother I had. I always wondered if she felt embarrassed. I'm sure she did. My mom had a lot of regulars too that would only stand in her line to be assisted only by her. Some of them were even some nice looking and kind men that often would try and ask her out. I often wonder if they asked her any questions about her appearance this particular day? About the obvious abuse? I wonder what she would say. My heart aches whenever I think about it all. Its still very painful for me.

This abuse went on for a long time. I can recall numerous incidents where my mom was abused and suffered tremendously at the hands of my father. Of course, my mom didn't want any of my friends to come over and see her that way. So again, no play dates or sleepovers for me. Eventually, I think I was about 9 or 10 when my mom had had enough. She divorced my dad. HALLELUJAH! ***Best day of my childhood life!***** When everything was finalized my mom, my brother and I moved out of "the house of torture" off 4th and Pierce to a bright new peaceful home

Mrs. Nakisha S. James

right on 11th Ave. Yyyaaaayyy Momma! A new life and new beginning had begun for us! ***Sometimes NOT being married as parents is the best thing for the children***

THE EAST COAST WOES

My dad ended up moving away to the East Coast up to Baltimore, MD. After maybe a year of him moving there, my brother and I started going to visit him during our summer breaks from school. I wasn't afraid of my father from what I saw him do to my mom however those images never left my mind. Going to see him was okay because he was still my dad. I did have mixed feelings at first, but I wanted to see what the East Coast looked like. Those summers away in Maryland were nice. We would go up to Washington, DC and see the White House and the Monument. We visited many parks and carnivals as well. Eventually he began dating a young lady. She had a son and they would come with us during many of our family outings. I remember very clearly when I was 11 years old and we were out at one of the carnivals, something happened that changed my whole life! I guess it was a good thing that my dad's new girlfriend was with us on this outing because IT HAPPENED! Of all times and of all places I started my period! YIKES!! Now before this the only explanation I had about getting my period was from my clueless friends at school. And you can only imagine the things I was told! My mom had not discussed this "situation" with me. And I couldn't tell my dad. So, I told his girlfriend. She broke the news to him. We immediately left the carnival. They took

Mrs. Nakisha S. James

me home. I took a bath and she gave me some feminine pads and kind of explained to me how to use them. What an experience!

When we got back home to Gary, my mom sent me over to aunt Nae-Nae's. She sat me down and began to tell me about the birds and the bees. I really don't know what birds and what bees she was referring to at that time, but I listened. I remember her telling me that I could not hug or even look at a boy or I would have a baby! WHAT?!? I can't look at ANY boy!? What about my brother or my uncle?? Geeze! So here I am walking around trying not to make any type of eye contact with anyone of the male gender thinking that I would get pregnant. ***Mothers please be upfront and tell your daughters the REAL TRUTH about sex!*** But of course, on my own, I will soon find out this was not true at all! Keep Reading...

JUNIOR HIGH

Tolleston Middle School was one of the BEST schools in Gary. My 7th and 8th grade years here were some of the most memorable I have ever had in school! I loved the teachers. Mr. Whiteside taught math!! I hated math!! And when it came to it Mr. Whiteside he did not play! Rest in Paradise sir. I was on the cheerleading squad and the flag team. Blue Raider to my heart! I loved Tolleston.

The summer of my 8th grade year, I was about 14, and I was hanging with some friends out in the West Brook homes. This was a community of townhouses not

Mrs. Nakisha S. James

far from where I lived. A lot of my friends lived there. It wasn't too far from Tolleston either. Since my dad had moved back to the Midwest to Illinois from Maryland, my brother and I didn't go to the East Coast on our breaks anymore. This summer things would be very different. We will call him "Mr. New Edition" He lived in Westbrook. He was the cousin of one of my friends. He was light skinned with green eyes. He was a little older than I was too. So, when I found out he liked me I was flattered. I had kept hearing stories from all my friends about them and their boyfriends having sex and all their experiences. I was the only one in the "clique" that had not "DONE IT" yet. Remember I was scared to even LOOK at any boys. This would be the summer this all would change. A bunch of us went to Ralph's house. Ralph and I went upstairs to his room. And it happened. OMG it hurt so badly!! Because it was hurting, we did not continue for long. But that didn't matter to me. I was part of the "IN CROWD" now. Well not exactly. A few short weeks later I was supposed to start my period and NOTHING! I quickly found out that not only was I pregnant but many of my friends were LYING about really "DOING IT!" My mom obviously had been watching when I would get my cycle. When she saw that I had not gotten it, yet she began asking questions. And like any normal teenager.... I LIED! I told her anything that I could think of so she would not kill me. I felt so bad and disappointed in myself. Of course, eventually I had to tell my mother. But you just don't TELL a black mother from Gary that you are pregnant at the age of 14! I did what any smart girl would do. I wrote her a letter and left it on her bed to find and read. Then I went to hide in my room to wait for the beat down. If I had went to her and verbally told her then I would not be alive today to write this book! TRUE STORY!! My Momma didn't play!

Mrs. Nakisha S. James

17

My mom was calmer about it than I ever expected. God was working in my favor on this one! Her and a friend of hers took me to have an abortion and that was that. No more mention of it. But I quickly learned that there is more than looking at a boy that causes you to get pregnant! I also learned through this whole situation. ***not to follow the crowd. Stay true to your beliefs and morals. Be a leader not a follower.** It doesn't matter what everyone else is doing. And 99% of the time they aren't doing anything at all. People.... especially teenagers LIE!!!

Now let me go back and say that as a child I was not raised up in church. I explained what my childhood household was like earlier in this chapter. I did not know or realize until I got much older that having an abortion was a sin against God. When I got pregnant, I was only 14 and still only a baby myself. I had a whole lot of growing up still to do. But I did not know that the event that would take place just one year later would make me grow up even faster than I anticipated and very much closer to God. Keep Reading...

Mrs. Nakisha S. James

What I Gained – Lesson 1

> *It's not always the men in the family that you have to watch around your little girls.

The stigma has been that it's always men who molest little girls. That's not always the case. You must be cognizant about anyone you let be around your children. Family or friends, men or women, boys or girls it really does not matter the age or the gender. Be careful. Protect your

> *This was one of those things that you just didn't talk about.

I cannot speak for every African American household but I do know that there are just some things you do not talk about in a "Black" home. This was one of them. I have no idea why things are like this, but things have been this way since the beginning of time. And these "secret" events plague a lot of little black girls that feel just like I felt..."Nobody would believe me anyway." Now that I am an adult and I have 2 little girls (and this goes for my 2 sons as well) I make sure that we have an open dialogue about sex and their bodies and about anyone touching them in any inappropriate way. I am making sure they do not grow up and have to live with something that happened to them when they were younger, and it is affects them when they become adults.

Mrs. Nakisha S. James

Kids are young but far from naïve.

Children are much smarter than what we give them credit for. Drugs were not "discussed" at my home, but I clearly knew what they were and why I could not have any friends over. I never judged my parents for what they did but of course I was not happy with not being able to have any friends over. I learned now as an adult and a mother of my own children, be very careful of what you show your children because it will follow them for the rest of their life.

Our past may not dictate our future but it sure does play a major part.

My mother was one of the strongest women on the planet! All that she went through on a day to day basis and she still managed to get up every morning and go to work. She had two babies to take care of. Some women might have taken a leave of absence or some PTO time....not Brenda. So that's where I get it from? *smile

Best day of my childhood life!

In many cases divorce is much better than staying married. Many couples stay together for the kids but many times the kids wish you would just go your separate ways. It can turn out to be a win–win for everyone. Maybe my brother and I would have never visited those places on the East Coast and had those educational experiences had not my parents gotten divorced. Furthermore, by no means should

Mrs. Nakisha S. James

any woman (man) have to endure any abuse by their spouse or significant other! This affects your children for the rest of their lives.

> *Mothers please be upfront and tell your daughters the truth about sex!*

I CAN NOT STRESS THIS ENOUGH! Mothers PLEASE be honest and tell your little girls about their period and ALL that comes along with it when they get it. Don't beat around the bush or be embarrassed to talk to them. And if you feel like you simply can not do it then please have their doctor explain it. But please do not give them false information or rely on the schools to teach them. It may save you from an early pregnancy/abortion later. I'm just saying

> *Do not to follow the crowd. Stay true to your beliefs and morals. Be a leader not a follower.*

Don't follow the crowd. Be a leader. Always stay true to yourself and your morals. Many times, when you hear that everyone else is doing something...9 times out of 10 no one is doing whatever that "something" is. Trust your gut. Listen to that little voice when it tells you something isn't right. It just may be your saving grace later.

Mrs. Nakisha S. James

CHAPTER 2

Chemistry Class

NOT SO HAPPY HOLIDAYS

After the pregnancy and the abortion, I didn't know what was going to happen to me. Was my Mom going to put me on punishment for the rest of my life? Would she kill me and hide my body? I just knew I would not see the light of day anymore. ***But when you make adult decisions/choices you better be ready for the adult consequences.** I wasn't sure if I was ready.

I was now 15 and starting high school. Horace Mann High School was THEE BEST high school in Gary at that time. Some people would disagree and say West Side, Or Roosevelt was the best. But we all know the truth. (Smile) Horace Mann was also the same high school my parents attended, my aunts and uncles, and my cousins. I guess you can say it was all in the family. While I attended there, I was

Mrs. Nakisha S. James

fortunate enough to be taught by some of the same teachers that my parents also had back during their high school days.

Freshman year was the best. I made the Freshman cheerleading squad. This is where I met my first set of sisters. Princess, Vanessa, Deidre, Tameka, Kellie, and Francis. I love these ladies to life! We all are still friends 30+ years later. Many of my friends from Tolleston Middle School came to Horace Mann as well. I also made a lot of new friends. One new friend was a boy by the name of John "Jay" Lucas. He was a junior when I got to Horace Mann. He was on the basketball and football team. One day one of his friends approached me and said that Jay liked me. WWHHAATTT?? Little ole freshman me? I was flattered. He was an upper classman so why would he like me? I was so scared. I just began to gain my Mom's trust back and now here he comes. I was not trying to get pregnant again and disappoint my Mom all over again. But he was so cute!

We began to talk. Come to find out his parents also went to Horace Mann with my parents. Again, all in the family. We "dated" all of my freshman and Sophomore years at Horace Mann. I was too young to actually "go out" on any dates so we mostly just talked on the phone and saw each other at school. Because I was on the cheer squad I would also see him during all the basketball and football games. I remember back in Gary we used to have this thing called the Football-O-Rama. It was basically like a football classic but on a high school level. We used to have tons of fun there. The best part was riding on the bus with the teams. Jay and I would try and sit next to each other but Ms. Black, our cheerleading coach, wasn't having that! Those were some good times. I guess you can say since Jay was my first true

Mrs. Nakisha S. James

boyfriend so that makes him my first love. He's doing very well today. He's with two beautiful babies. Thanks for the great high school memories J-Luc!

It was January 7, 1992. I remember this day as if it happened just yesterday. The day my entire life would change. A week or so before, something unreal had taken place. It was Christmas 1991. My mom, myself, my brother, AND my dad was all together again. WHAAATTT!?!? Seems that my parents had been talking and decided to give it another shot. I was not 100% thrilled about this at all! This was the first Christmas in years that we all were together. We were in IL at my dad's apartment. I must be honest; this was not the greatest time for me. All I could remember from previous experiences was when my mom and dad were "together", usually my mom would end up with a black eye. I was terrified. As the night fell my parents slept in my dad's room and my brother and I slept out in the living room. Well he slept....I stayed up most of the night up afraid I would hear cursing and fighting.

Christmas day came and went. Gifts were exchanged. We had dinner. All seemed to be going okay. On December 31, 1991, New Years Eve, my mom and dad decide to go out to a party. I remember my brother and I were being dropped of to our cousin's house. They were not going to leave us at home alone on New Year's Eve! Not in Gary, IN! Now remember currently I am 15 years old. Well pass the baby years. But I cried all the way to my cousin's home. I cried when we went inside. I cried like a 2-year-old and begged my mom not to go out with my dad. I was terrified that something bad was going to happen. I guess my big baby tears meant absolutely nothing because she went anyway. I prayed to God "PLEASE DON'T LET ANYTHING HAPPEN TO MY MOMMY!" I was so terrified once again! God does

Mrs. Nakisha S. James

answer prayers! She came back in one piece. What a relief. It seemed like they were on the path of "working things out." I really did not want that. I was happy with just my mom, my brother and myself in our nice little home on 11th Ave. Needless to say, I was ecstatic my mom came back from the party in one piece and not all battered and bruised but I really didn't enjoy one minute of the coming in of the new year 1992. And it was about to get worse. Keep Reading...

CHEMISTRY CLASS

I was in Chemistry class, right after lunch, at Horace Mann High School. It was my sophomore year. I remember this day so well because I absolutely hated Chemistry! I hated every Science, but Chemistry had to be the worse! I was (and still am) and English and Literature girl. Anything to do with numbers or formulas was just not my cup of tea. But tell me to read something or write a paper then you got me! I remember sitting at my desk and complaining in my head how bad this class was for me. I remember thinking "What's the point of learning all this stuff when I know I would probably never use any of it once I graduate high school!?" I was so in a funk. Then the classroom door opens. One of the office staff comes in. "Nakisha Rayford please gather your things and come with me." Me? What I do? I know I don't like this class but am I in trouble for that?? Did they hear me mumbling about hating Chemistry?! I never got into trouble or was called out of the class, so I was nervous. What was going on??

Mrs. Nakisha S. James

*As much as I hated Chemistry class, I found out that things can be much worse. Things are not always as bad as what they seem

I gathered my things and I stepped out into the hall where my Aunt Nae-Nae was standing with uncontrollable tears in her eyes. So of course, I asked "WHAT'S WRONG???" She could barely even talk to get the words out to tell me. All I could make out of what she was saying was "your mother." I was led downstairs to my locker to get my coat and the rest of my belongings. My aunt signed me out of school, and we headed over to Methodist Hospital.

When I walked in the ER the waiting area was full of our family and friends. All of them had tears and sadness all over their faces. My Grannie worked at Methodist as a housekeeper. They lead me toward the back where the rooms were and there was my Grannie surrounded by many of her co-workers. She also was crying and so was her co-workers. So now I am shaking and wondering what is going on!? I was led further back to the room my mom was in. I really didn't know what to expect but from the tears and the sadness of everyone I knew it wasn't good. I have never been more scared in all my life. The curtain opened and there she was. My mom was laying there…tubes everywhere, machines and beeping noises. All the stuff I had only seen up until this point on television. But it was real, and it was happening to my mom. I moved closer. I touch her hand. It's was so cold. I start to cry and I yell "MOMMA, IT'S KISHA! MOMMA, MOMMA, MOMMA, IT'S ME KISHA!" No answer. I begin to cry harder. I yell louder, "MOMMA….MOMMA….IT'S KISHA MOMMA! WAKE UP!" Oh my God this was not happening to me.

Mrs. Nakisha S. James

They took me back out to the waiting area. Everyone saw my reaction and immediately tried to comfort me. I don't even recall where my brother was during all of this. Suddenly, the ER outside doors slide open. It's my dad. They took him back to see my mom. Not even five minutes later I see him running out of the hospital into the parking lot. He could not handle seeing my mom that way.

After sitting in the ER waiting area for some time, all the young people were sent across the street to my Aunt Nae Nae's home. None of us had eaten anything so they thought it would be best for us to leave and get some food. I was too scared to eat. That vision of my mom laying there kept flashing before my eyes. I sat in one spot the whole time when I remember I heard the door open. It's maybe 10pm now. My aunt walks in and all I can hear her screaming is "MY SISTER IS GONE....I HAVE NO MORE SISTERS....BOTH OF MY SISTERS ARE GONE!" Just two years earlier my other Aunt Thelma (yes, the same aunt that lived with my Grannie in the home on 4th and Buchanan) had passed away. My Nae-Nae's neighbor Debra was with her. She saw me sitting on the couch. She came over to me and hugged me and told me my mom had passed away. I pushed her off me and told her she was a lie! I told her my mom was alive and that she was coming to pick me and my brother up any minute as usual. She kept trying to grab me and console me and I was not trying to hear any of it! But I knew. Deep down I knew. When I touched my mom's cold hand I knew. But I didn't want to believe it. Again, this could not be happening to me!

Within minutes the apartment was full of friends and family all with tears in their eyes. It was so unreal. My Dad arrived and I didn't know how to feel. All I could think about was all the years of abuse she endured with him and now she was

Mrs. Nakisha S. James

gone. I was so lost and confused. I was so hurt and sad. The worst feeling, I have ever felt. This was not what a 15-year-old is supposed to go through. I found out later that my mom had suffered a brain aneurysm and a stroke which she did not recover from. I miss her so much. Rest in paradise Momma.***Here today....gone today. Live every minute of your life like it is your last because he just might be. Laugh often. Love everyone. Leave a legacy.**

Mrs. Nakisha S. James

28

What I Gained – Lesson 2

> *But when you make adult decisions/choices you better be ready for the adult consequences*

When I decided to have sex at the age of 14, to follow behind my lying friends, I learned really fast that every decision I make will have a consequence. Just so happened, this consequence could have changed my entire life. I would have become a mother at the age of 14. Now, being a mom of 4, I could not even imagine how I would have been anybody's mother at 14! Be careful of the crowd that you follow and every decision that you make. Because, in the end, YOU AND ONLY YOU have to deal with the consequences.

> *As much as I hated Chemistry class, I found out that things can be much worse. Things are not always as bad as what they seem*

Even when we feel we are in the worse predicament ever things can ALWAYS be worse. I found this out at age 15. I would have taken a million Chemistry classes and loved them if I could have not lost my mom that day. Always be thankful and grateful for your life everyday no matter what stage your life is in. Still until this day I believe whole heartedly God was trying to tell my mother not to go backwards and return to the abuse she once endured with my father. She wasn't listening so he took her under his arm and led her to safety. He saved her life by taking her life.

Mrs. Nakisha S. James

Here today....gone today. Live each and every minute of your life like it is your last because he just might be. Laugh often. Love everyone. Leave a legacy.

Losing my mom at such a young age really made me see life through a different set of eyes. Remembering all that she had been through and endured in the short 35 years she lived. Now with 2 daughters and 2 sons of my own, it is my destiny to make sure that I leave a positive impact on their lives and a legacy for them to continue for future generations.

Mrs. Nakisha S. James

CHAPTER 3

Tough Transitions

LIFE WITHOUT MA

Brenda Burnetta Rayford. My Momma. Gone but you will never be forgotten. You gave me life and I had the pleasure of seeing your beautiful face everyday for 15 years. And for that I am so grateful. But now I had to move on with life without you. What a tough pill to swallow. Where do I start? What do I do? Where does it begin? Where would my brother and I live? Who would take care of us now? All these questions I had. I wanted to stay in Gary with my Aunt Nae Nae. My dad wanted my brother and I to move and stay with him in Illinois. Through a court battle my dad gained custody of me and my brother. ***My mom didn't have a WILL or anything in place that would suggest her last wishes for her children.** So from January 1992 until the end of the school year in May 1992, my brother and I stayed with my dad's sister, our other aunt, over on 3rd and Chase Street. My dad allowed us to stay in Gary so that we could finish out that school year. I was in the 10th grade at Horace Mann High School. I had friends there that I have had since Kindergarten.

Mrs. Nakisha S. James

Friends I was on the cheerleading squad with, played double dutch with. I knew their moms and their moms knew me and my mom. Even some of my teachers I had at Horace Mann also taught my mom and dad. I was known throughout the school and my community. My brother was just finishing 8th grade at Tolleston Middle School. Throughout our whole lives all we knew was the streets of Gary, Indiana. That was about to change real soon!

Every weekend my dad would come to Gary and pick my brother and I up from his sister's house where we were staying. We would then ride over to Illinois to look at homes for us to move into. After a while all the houses started to look alike to me. Additionally, I was still in total disbelief that my mom was gone and my brother and I was about to be uprooted and move into a totally different environment. Finally, we decided on a home located in Berkeley, IL. It was a very nice neighborhood. It was mostly Caucasian which was nothing like the neighborhoods we grew up in in Gary. It was a 2-story home with a basement and a huge backyard. Coming from where I come from it was like a house you would only see on television. It wasn't too far from Proviso West High School located in Hillside, IL. This school was 3 times the size of Horace Mann. I just knew I would get lost every day. Also, no one would know me here. I was a brand-new face, unlike what I had back in Gary. Even though I was now in my junior year of high school I felt like a freshman all over again.

The summer of 1992 came, and we moved into our new home. Bye bye Gary and Horace Mann. Also, bye bye from living with a woman to now living with a man....my dad....who I had not shared a home within many years. BIG TRANSITION! I

Mrs. Nakisha S. James

soon found out that being the only female in the home meant having many obligations. My dad did cook sometimes but I had to learn to make a quick meal myself. Laundry, grocery shopping, cleaning, all the things I did WITH my mom, I now had to do on my own. I was 16 so it was okay. I needed to learn to do these things on my own. It was a tough transition but also a big learning experience for me. I grew up much faster than I had anticipated. Keep Reading...

FIRST DAY AT P-DUB (PROVISO WEST HIGH SCHOOL)

Geeze Louise!!!! I felt like I was an ant walking through a major city as I walked through the hallways of Proviso West High School. This school was HUGE!!! Like 3 times the size of Horace Mann High. It was like being a freshman all over again. Each grade had a color badge you had to wear while you were inside the school. If I remember yellow was freshman, black was sophomore, green was junior and red was senior. What a surprise to everyone's face that this new girl was walking through the halls with this GRREN ID on. I mean she's clearly a freshman. Too funny! There were so many classes and halls and sections to this school. And just like back home where I grew up with a group of friends, there were many kids here that grew up together and formed "groups" of friends or "cliques" as they were called. I really felt like an outcast on many days.

Mrs. Nakisha S. James

I didn't talk a whole lot. I pretty much stayed to myself. Some of the other students thought I was mean and stuck up, but the truth of the matter is I had quite a bit going on. ***Never judge a book/person by it's cover...you never know what they may be going through.** As the days and weeks went on, and I begin to learn my way around, I made some friends. Anleeta, Camesia, Latoya, Abbie, Shantel, Kira just to name a few. I felt like I was starting my school life all over again as if I was back in Kindergarten. The classes were cool, once I found out how to get to all of them. The lunch times were interesting. Everything was just different, and I had to learn the ropes.

SENIOR YEAR

I got through the first year at Proviso West. WHEW!! I must admit it was very rocky at first but turned out to be great toward the end. I had made tons of friends and I had learned my new area very well. My junior year I really didn't do too much. Now homecoming, prom, graduation, and all that comes along with being a senior was right in front of me. And I was ready to get this year started. I still had the heartbreak of losing my mom, but I was really going to go out and try to enjoy my last year of high school. I begin going out with friends and attending the school sporting events and dances. I even ran for Homecoming queen and came out 1st runner up. WHAT!? The new girl?! Things were going well. I even had a boyfriend. His name was Keith. He was tall and played on the football team. He was well known at the school. Things were good. I loved my new school, my new friends and my new

Mrs. Nakisha S. James

life. I went to prom, I graduated and walked across the stage, and I was on my way to college. My mom would have been so proud.

Mrs. Nakisha S. James

What I Gained – Lesson 3

> *My mom didn't have a WILL or anything in place that would suggest her last wishes for her children.*

After going through this ordeal with losing my mom and how it affected my brother and I, I promised myself that when I had children of my own that I would be sure to have some documents in place for my family. Thank God that a service called LegalShield came into my life that gave me the opportunity to get these documents completed. Now my Last Will and Testament, my Living Will, and my Health Care Directives are all documented. I pray that all my friends that have children learn from my experience and do the same. I sleep better at night knowing I have these things in place for my family.

> *Never judge a book/person by it's cover...you never know what they may be going through*

Many times, we encounter people and they may look mean in the face or they may not say good morning when you speak to them. It's possible they may be dealing with something traumatic. This does not mean that they are rude or inconsiderate individuals. We all deal with "life" differently. All that I was dealing with as a teen was sometimes unbearable, and it showed on my face and in my

Mrs. Nakisha S. James

attitude towards other people. But as time passed and I began to deal with the situation my fellow students and now good friends see that I am the silliest person ever! So, the next time you encounter someone like this just think before you judge.

Mrs. Nakisha S. James

CHAPTER 4

SIUC Shenanigans

SCHNEIDER HALL

It's now the summer of 1994. Southern Illinois University Carbondale here I come! I was now 18 years old and about to be on my own as a college student. I was too excited. Another new beginning with new experiences and meeting more new people. I could get used to this! August came and we drove down to SIUC to get me all settled in my new dorm. It was about a 6-hour drive. There were cars and new freshman everywhere! I didn't feel like the one and only new girl anymore like I did back in high school. There were a bunch of us this time. We unloaded all my things out of the car and headed up to my room. Schneider Hall...I will never forget. My room mate had not made it there yet, so I chose my side of the room and began unpacking and getting settled in. I was a big balloon fan and so over the years I had deflated and kept a bunch of the foil balloons I had received for birthdays and other special events in my life. I began hanging them on my side of the room. After a couple hours of that, we left to grab something to eat. Then it was time for them to head back up to Berkeley. There wasn't really a sad goodbye like some college students have when they are being dropped off to school. I just kept thinking I am really on my own?! Once my dad left, I began to meet other students in my building and seeing their moms AND dads with them. I began to think about my mom and how I wished she was there to see me off. She was there...in my heart. It still wasn't the same. But I knew things were going to be just fine...so I thought. Keep Reading...

ROOMATE 1...THEN 2...THEN 3...

Going away to college was a life altering experience for me to say the least. There were people there of all shades, colors, backgrounds, ethnicities, and cultures. Remember I was just a black girl from predominately black Gary, Indiana so all of this was quite new to me. After a while my roommate finally arrived. We will call her "Ce-Ce" She was also African American. But she was much different than other African American girls I had ever met. She wore a lot of black. Even her nail polish and lipstick were always black. She had a nose piercing and wore her hair short. When she began to get settled and unpack, I noticed she hung up posters of some rock bands she liked. Bands like Guns and Roses, Rage Against the Machine....none of the groups or bands I had ever heard of or were familiar with. She intrigued me. We got along well. At least that's what I thought.

Mrs. Nakisha S. James

One afternoon I was taking a shower. Our room was a suite, so the shower was in the middle between our room and the room next door. I guess "Ce-Ce" didn't realize it was me in the bathroom and not our suite mate. I heard her and some of her friends talking. Some of her comments were heartbreaking. She made a comment about some jeans in my closet and showed her friends "She has every color...that is so ghetto" She made comments about the music I liked "And that jungle music that she plays" Jungle music?? So, R Kelly is considered jungle music. "And look at all the balloons on the wall like who does that" When I stepped out of the bathroom all conversation had ceased. I didn't say a word but I did learn that day that ***Just because they are same race or color as you are does not mean that they see things the same as you do.** I never said anything to her about her comments. Those were her thoughts and her personal feelings and so I left it as that. "Ce-Ce" didn't come back the next semester. Thank God! Not that I didn't like her, but I was just so ashamed and shocked how one sister could hate on another sister so bluntly. So now on to roommate #2...

We will call her "Kay" She was also African American. Thin girl but had a lot of mouth. She was not afraid to say what she felt to whoever she felt. She and I got along well though. We pretty much shared the entire room. There wasn't really her side and my side.

Her cousin's dorm room was right across the hall from our dorm room, so we all became good friends. Kay had a boyfriend that did not attend school there at SIUC. At first, he would come to visit maybe every other weekend, then it was every weekend, then it was like he had moved in. He was there all the time. Imagine how

Mrs. Nakisha S. James

uncomfortable that is for me to come in from class and wanting to take a shower or relax and there's this guy there that doesn't belong. That went on for some time. I didn't say anything. I mean I was seeing someone as well but he was a student there so he would come over to our room, but he also would leave and go back to his own dorm. One fine day I think I had had enough. I mentioned her boyfriend being in our dorm. Why did I do that?! As I mentioned earlier in the chapter "Kay" had a mouth on her! An argument began. She mentioned my boyfriend being there and her not having a problem with him so I should not have a problem with hers being there. This argument got very heated. So heated that her cousin across the hall and some other girls on the floor heard us. They came in our room and tried to calm us down. Names were called and words were exchanged between the both of us. But when Kay uttered the words "YOUR MOTHER IS A BITCH!" OOOOOHHHHH why Jesus!!!! Now mind you she knew my mom was deceased. Another death was about to take place that day! I instantly saw red and I tried my best to get to her so I can put my hands around her neck. But with all the people in our room no one would let her, or I near each other. ***I don't know who said words will never hurt you because that day those words she said stung me to my core.** They separated us out of the dorm room. I never saw Kay again after that. I ended up having a room by myself for the rest of the semester. I started to believe that probably was the best thing because me and roommates just didn't seem to click. But then I got roommate #3.......

It is now my third semester at SIUC and I have already gone through 2 roommates. Having a dorm room all to myself had its advantages but at times I did wish I had someone there to laugh and joke with. I didn't have any sisters growing up so I kind of missed that. But I sure did not want any of the drama I had the last 2

Mrs. Nakisha S. James

semesters. Then roommate #3, Courtney, came. Lord please don't let her hate my clothes or my "jungle music" or call my mother out of her name because if so, I'm going to jail so help me Jesus!! God must have been on my side this time! Courtney was, and still is, an absolutely doll!! She was gorgeous inside and out. Very down to earth and we became more than friends...we are now sisters! We never had 1 argument about anything. She also had a guy she was seeing on campus but we both respected each other's privacy. She has been in my life ever since those college days back at SIUC and I love her to pieces. *** I guess what they say is true that the third time is the charm.**

ACADEMIC WARNING

After all the hurt I endured with losing my mom and then all the drama I had with my roommates in college my grades showed it all. They were not the worst but they sure were not my best. I just had so much on my mind and on my chest that I really had no clue how to process it all. I met another group of ladies on campus. They were cool and we got along well. I remember we had decided that we were going to create our own "sorority." We had our little cat call and everything all ready to go. But that never happened. There was this other group of ladies that also lived in Schneider Hall. That group of girls I had become close with didn't care too much for this "clique." Now anyone who knows me knows that I am and always have been a no nonsense no drama young lady. I knew trouble was brewing when these two groups begin to argue back and forth every time they saw each other on campus. One

Mrs. Nakisha S. James

evening we were all sitting around chit chatting in Schneider Hall. One of the young ladies from my group of friends suggested that we all go down to the floor where the other group of ladies were and fight them. You know, show them once and for all who's Queen! I didn't want to go. I try my best to stay away from trouble...but these were my "friends" right? So, guess what...we all went onto their floor and there they were. I honestly can't remember who hit who first, but I do remember there was some mace sprayed and it was just a mess. After it was all over, we all scattered. My room was right upstairs so that's where I went. Weeks passed. I stopped hanging with those ladies. After that semester I ended up going home and leaving SIUC because of my grades. Not soon after I made it back to Berkeley a call from the SIUC police came to my house. It seems that there was a warrant for my arrest for the fight that took place just a few weeks prior. My dad was talking to them trying to get the details. My heart was pounding in my chest. Yes, I was there and I saw everything but not once did I throw any punches or spray any mace. I didn't hit anyone. I didn't dislike any of these girls but I was guilty by association and because my face was known to associate with those girls I was treated just as if I had been involved. Long story short, the other girls did have to go to court and they told them I was not involved. Thank God for honesty! But I did learn that day ***if you follow the wrong crowd you will get negative results.** Whew Lord what more drama could happen in my life!? Well....Keep Reading

Mrs. Nakisha S. James

43

What I Gained – Lesson 4

> **Just because they are same race or color as you are does not mean that they see things the same as you do*

Growing up in Gary, all we had were Black...African American people all around us. It was very seldom that I saw anyone outside of my race in Gary. I really had not experienced any type of racism growing up. Then when we moved to Berkeley (which at the time was predominantly all white) there was a little bit of it. But never ever had I experienced it from someone who looked just like me. Same color as me. How can you be racist against your own? I learned that day that not everyone loves themselves or the skin they are in so don't always look for them to love you. Have a diverse group of friends.

> **I don't know who ever said words will never hurt you because that day those words she said stung me to my core*

Sticks and stones may break my bones but......how many times have we heard this as a child? Why did they teach us this lie! Words definitely do hurt! And some words hurt so bad they don't ever heal. Back then...25 years ago when this took place...Oh I would have went to jail because of what she said. Over some WORDS. Everyone has a threshold and a "I SEE RED" button. And if pushed at the right time

Mrs. Nakisha S. James

there's no telling what will happen. Now today if someone was to call me out my name or my mom, I would just look at them with a look of stupidity. That's because I have grown and matured to know that people who do that have some issues of their own.

I guess what they say is true that the third time is the charm.

After going through 2 roommates in under a year I did start to look at myself and wonder what in the world was wrong with me!? Am I that bad of a person? Am I that hard to get along with? So, when Courtney came, I was terrified! Either she was going to kill me or I was going to kill her I knew it!! I should not have prejudged! I learned even though we go through life and we all have our ups and downs and good and bad, we should never put what we have experienced on the next person that comes into our lives. All our baggage and extra weight was not the fault of the new person. I am so happy I realized that quickly and I gained a sister because of it. Love you to pieces Courtney!

if you follow the wrong crowd you will get negative results

There was a game we used to play called Follow the Leader as a kid. Or the game Simon Says. These games taught us how to follow someone else's lead and not our own. These games some how registered with us throughout our lives and have caused many people to not know how to function without someone telling them

Mrs. Nakisha S. James

what to do. In my case I didn't want to look like the chicken out the group and stay back. So, I went. And it almost cost me my life. What if they had not said I wasn't involved and I was arrested? That would have been a mark on my record for the rest of my life. Thank God for FAVOR! I learned that day to go with your gut! Never follow a group that you know is up to something that you morally are against. It will save you and your blood pressure!

Mrs. Nakisha S. James

CHAPTER 5

Heartbreak before the Husband

THE LIGHT SKINNED GUY

All women go through it. You meet that one guy and you swear he is the one. Then slowly but surely you realize he's as crazy as a betsy bug! Now I don't have a clue what a betsy bug is but if it's as crazy as any of my Ex's he needs a bit of therapy. But all of this adds up to a well-rounded young woman who learns each encounter was apart of her makeup. Let's start shall we...

First there was the light skinned guy...we'll call him MR. PLAYBOY. He was tall with a bald head and wore hazel contacts. (Don't judge me and this choice in a guy, I was young! LOL!) I met him after only a week or so of being on campus at SIUC. Him and his group of friends were well known around the yard. He and I began to talk and get to know each other more. Then after a few months, things got a bit serious. At least I thought they were. I didn't know he had a girl and a baby back

Mrs. Nakisha S. James

home in Chicago. He would get phone calls when I was in his room and he would always try and play it off. Finally, I asked about one of the calls. He confessed that yes, he had a son but he was not with the mom anymore. He swore to the hills that I was the only lady in his life. I believed him. And time moved on. Another time I was in his room just chilling and there was a knock on the door. He answered. It was another girl. He stepped outside to talk to her. He was out there for quite some time. I went to look out the door and no one was out there. When he finally came back, I asked, "So where did you and her go?" He brushed it off and said, "I just walked her down to the elevator so she could go home." I asked, "Who is she and what did she want with you?" His response "She asked about work from one of our classes we have together." Now mind you this dude barely went to class so how can someone come and ask YOU OF ALL PEOPLE anything about the work from class. But I let that go and time went on. Christmas break came. We both went back home to be with family. I don't believe we saw each other none of the break. School was back in session and all was well. Then it was time for Spring break. I went over to MR. PLAYBOY's home back in Chicago. He sat me down and told me that the same girl, the girl he said that he was not with, the mother of his son, the one that kept calling him while he was at school, was now pregnant with his SECOND child. WHAT!!!!???? So, this is why I didn't see you during the Christmas break because you were real busy populating the earth! We got into a real heated argument! So heated his aunt heard us and came to diffuse the situation. ***Always listen to your gut...for women it's called intuition.** I knew he was still with her...I JUST KNEW IT but I didn't listen to that little voice. He begged and pleaded that I stick with him and not leave him. I was so hurt.

Mrs. Nakisha S. James

Time went on. She had her baby. He kept calling me and would not let me be. I did care a great deal for him so we began talking again. But the more and more we talked and tried to move forward I knew he was no good for me. See I listened to that voice that second time. After some time, he went his way and I went mine. But I will say I learned a lot from this relationship. I realized after we split that I went back to him and tried to make it work because I was missing love in my life. My mom was gone and my dad and I didn't have the best relationship so MR. PLAYBOY was all I had. So, I thought. Whatever he did I allowed it. Oh, and there were other women besides the Baby Momma too. Some would call my phone. I caught him on the phone sweet talking another one. Yeah it was a true dysfunctional relationship. But I learned what God was teaching me. Well...maybe...Keep reading...

THE RADIO PERSONALITY

Anyone who knows me knows that I'm like LL KOOL J "I CAN'T LIVE WITHOUT MY RADIO!" LOL!! I am a music fanatic. I go to sleep to it, wake up to it, I must have music on to do everything in my life. Whenever any of the radio shows would have an outside community event I was there! I remember meeting one of the most famous personalities at one of these events. We will call him MR. RADIO. He was tall, light skinned (I know...light skinned dudes....here we go again) and very handsome. We chit chatted at the event and exchanged numbers. I would come out to all the events I knew he would be hosting for his radio show. Sometimes he would be the guest "celebrity" host out at this club not too far by my apartment. After that

Mrs. Nakisha S. James

event he would stop by my home before he would head home. Crazy thing....I had never been to his home. Something isn't right here. (Intuition) All of our "dates" were at my home. I heard that voice telling me something's not right. Then that other voice saying "But this is MR. RADIO and he's so handsome and he's on the radio and.......I listened to that second voice. Time went on. About a year into this I get a phone call at work. It was a woman asking me questions about MR. RADIO. This really blindsided me. But the kicker is MR. RADIO was also on the phone. Oh Lord not again! As she and I talked back and forth MR. RADIO says to her "Babe I don't know who this woman is, I am not with her, she is someone I probably met doing a radio event." WHAT?!?!? ARE YOU FREAKING KIDDING ME!!!! Did he just say he didn't know who I was? Crushed again. Intuition. She asked had I ever been to his home because there are pictures of her everywhere. And I honestly had to tell her no I had never been to his home. And of course, MR. RADIO jumped right in and said, "See she's never been over to the house so how can we be seeing each other?" I hung up the phone. I left work. I went home and cried. How could I have been so stupid! Why didn't I see the signs? And I remembered the woman saying to me "He could never want you if you see me!" Obviously, she was right...he could never want me. Who wants me!? Nobody. Sometime later MR. RADIO tried to call and apologize. I wasn't buying it! He had already done the damage and some things "I'm sorry" just don't fix. So, there I was, heartbroken once again. So, what's a girl to do? I had to pull myself together and keep pushing. Another lesson learned right? Keep reading......

Mrs. Nakisha S. James

THE CHURCH GUY

A long time had passed after that last break up. After getting over that I just begin to bury myself in my job and I started school again. I also began going to church regularly. I knew that if I was to get anything out of all this drama, I needed God to answer some questions. I joined Rock of Ages Baptist Church in Maywood IL where the Pastor is Marvin E. Wiley. I LOVED my church!! I was there for 2 services some Sundays! I mean it wasn't like I had something else better to do so why not give the Lord some time. At "The Rock" all new members had to go through these New Members classes. Basically, every Sunday morning before service we would go and learn more about the church and its auxiliaries, what it meant to be saved, baptism, and a host of other Christian teachings. After the weeks of classes were over the church held a small graduation for all the students. At the graduation I met a young man. We will call him MR. RELIGION. A little taller than I was, very fit like he worked out, light brown completion (I was done with them light skinned jokers!) We sat next to one another at the graduation. We both got our certificates and enjoyed the ceremony. We talked for a while after everything was over and we exchanged numbers. Okay....I'm thinking....Lord I met the man IN CHURCH!! This one has GOT to be the one! We began talking over the phone quite often. Then we went out on quite a few dates. He was quite the gentleman, always opening the door for me and holding my hand. Very different from the last 2 I had dated! Of course, I am impressed. We did a lot together. And did I tell ya'll that he could cook too! He cooked many dinners at his Condo and always invited me over instead of me always

Mrs. Nakisha S. James

cooking and being at my home. Total 360 from what I had experienced before! This was perfect!! Two years......still doing well....so I thought. Keep Reading...

There were some things that I ignored that he would do because of course you have to take the good with the bad right? Wrong! There were many things that he wanted me to do that I just felt like a wife should do! Not just a girlfriend. And I'm talking some very explicit things that he would ask. I was always taught "Why would a man buy the cow if he can get the milk for free?" In other words, **Why would a man marry you if you are already playing the role of his wife.** But his thing was "Well how do I know that the person is the person that I want to marry if they can't fulfill my needs while we are dating?" Lord what have I gotten myself into? I must be very honest and admit that I did give in to SOME of his request....NOT ALL!! I mean he was such a gentleman and seem to have everything in his life going well which is what a woman is looking for in a man....right? But it seemed that that when I did give in to those things then he wanted more and demanded more. Wait a dog gone minute now!! What in tarnation do you think I am!? Then I found out something interesting about MR. RELIGION. Not only did he study Christianity, but he also was very heavy into other religions. He would read these writings from these other groups and begin to form his own way of living. He would pick and choose different "scriptures" from each and live according to ONLY those. Of course, only choosing the ones he liked. Which there is nothing wrong with that...if your mate is going along with that as well. And I was not! I stood by my Christian faith and I wasn't trying to here What Thus Said Farrakhan or Buddha, or anybody else! After so many disagreements over time MR. RELIGION began to pull away. We were still "dating" but not so serious as once before. The dates became few and far between.

Mrs. Nakisha S. James

So did the calls and house visits. So eventually we both called it quits. Obviously, it was for the best. I stood my ground on my Faith and I wasn't bulging! ***If you feel a certain way about something stand firm in your feeling. It's a reason why you have that feeling in the first place.*** If your beliefs and morals do not match that of the person you are dating, then run for the hills! There will always be conflict between two people that believe two totally different ways of living.

MR. RELIGION is now happily married. I'm glad that he was able to find someone that could be worthy of having his last name. After we had broken up, I WAS DONE!! So done with men and dating and all that. I was like if I couldn't even find "THE ONE" at church then I am just going to remain single for the rest of my life. So once again I buried myself in my work, my studies, and I remained committed to my church. At that time, I must honestly say I was the happiest I had been in a while. I came and went as I pleased. I wasn't worried about why "so and so" not calling me. I even went out to eat and to the movies alone...just me, myself, and I. And it was great!! But you know you always have that one friend that thinks every woman needs a man? Yeah, I had one of them....Keep Reading....

THE BLIND DATE

Let me tell you about my good dear friend Mrs. Ross. She and I worked together at Zurich Life back in Hoffman Estates, IL. She was married with children and so she believed that every woman needed to be married with some babies. We

Mrs. Nakisha S. James

had been friends for a while and so she'd seen what happened with Mr. Radio and The Church guy. Epic fails! One day she comes to me at work and says "Kisha, I know that you are doing your own thing and being single but you still need to eat...so why not eat out on a date with a man?" I didn't want any parts of any of that "dating" stuff. I was so good being alone. But my friend didn't believe me. A little time had passed and Mrs. Ross comes to me and says, "I have a guy for you!" Lord Jesus why!?! She tells me he works with her husband. This guy is tall, dark, and looks just like Morris Chestnut. SAY WHAT SAY WHO?! Now hold on because ain't a man alive as PHYNE as Morris Chestnut!! (At least that's what I thought at that time) So I asked my friend had she seen this guy or is she going by what her husband is telling her. She had not laid any eyes on him ever. So now I am definitely not interested! Then she tells me she had given her husband my number to give to him. WHAT?! Again, Lord Jesus WHY!?! Mrs. Ross says to me "You are a beautiful woman and any man would be lucky to have you. Just talk to the guy, you never know what may happen." But looking how my luck with men had been so far, I kind of had an idea what would happen. Sigh!

Some time had passed and no call from Mr. Morris. Mrs. Ross would ask me everyday "DID HE CALL...DID HE CALL?" Nope was always my response. And I wasn't mad that he hadn't. I was still doing me. She asked her husband to ask him why he had not called me. Come to find out he had written my name on a paper bag that he threw away by mistake. YES!! I was free!! Nope not at all. Mrs. Ross told her husband to get his number for me and I would call him. Sigh! It took me a while but I did call. I guess I didn't want to be rude. He answered. I introduced myself. It was kind of awkward. I'd never done anything like this before but I learned that **to have**

Mrs. Nakisha S. James

54

something you've never had you must do something you've never done. The conversation continued. I want to say we talked for about an hour. I found out not only did he work with Mr. Ross but he also was a preacher. Another church guy....Good Jesus help me! So of course, all kind of mixed feelings begin to build up in me. We talked and talked and talked some more. We talked over the phone for about 2 months. We had talked about everything under the sun and still had not laid eyes on one another. No pictures or anything. I did tell him that I was told he resembled Morris Chestnut. He told me that he was told I resembled Nia Long. Too funny! So now of course we are both anxious to see each other. To see if what we were told was true.

After digging into each other's lives for the past two months Mr. Chestnut decided to officially ask me out. Ooooh...like a date? Ummm...but you are still a stranger...kind of. He suggested we meet in a wide-open public place. After much contemplating I finally agreed. After work on a Friday I drove to Portillo's (a popular Chicago eatery) on Cicero way south away from my home in Carol Stream. I parked outside. He called and asked me what color and what kind of car I was in. I told him. Then a few minutes later a car pulls up right beside me and sits there. The windows were so dark tented I could not see inside the car. No one gets out for seemed like 5 minutes. So now all kind of crazy thoughts are running through my head. Is this him? He's in there plotting to kill me right here in Portillo's parking lot. Thank God I had already told Mrs. Ross and 3 other people where I was going so if I came up missing, they would know where to start the search. Then the door opened...this guy stepped out....LORD be some glasses because I know I am not seeing what I am seeing!

Mrs. Nakisha S. James

He opens my passenger door and gets in....it was Morris! Well...not exactly but you could not get any closer resemblance! Very tall...6'3", dark chocolate skin (I have never dated anyone dark so this was new), a gorgeous smile, and he smelled so good!!! God now stop playing you know I am sensitive right now! When he gets in and sees me the first thing he says is "You do look like Nia Long!" HA! And my response was "And you look like Morris Chestnut!" WOW! So not only had we become friends after talking over the phone for nearly 3 months but now to put the face with the voice was great! We go inside to eat. I quickly found that he is quite the comedian as well! He had me laughing from the time we went in and the whole time we sat to eat. We sat and talked and ate and talked some more. After we were done with our meal, we went next door to play some miniature golf. Something I had never played before. It was a lot of fun. It was getting late and time for me to head back over to my side of town. We walked back over to where my car was parked. We said our goodbyes and off I went. It was a nice night. He called me later when I had made it home and we talked again for some hours. I'm not going to get excited about this one because we see what happened from my previous relationships. But.......Keep Reading...

Mrs. Nakisha S. James

What I Gained – Lesson 5

*Always listen to your gut...for women it's called intuition

All girls/women have this inner voice. It is called our women's intuition. And yes, IT IS REAL! Sometimes it can be as loud as a bullhorn telling us to PAUSE! Then other times it can be just a whisper telling us to rethink that decision. Either way a lot of times us women ignore that voice. We lead and make our decisions with our emotions instead. Not saying that is totally bad but it can be beneficial in the long wrong to listen to your intuition. If I had listened to my inner voice....intuition during this time in my life then maybe I could have avoided a lot of pain.

*Why would a man marry you if you are already playing the role of his wife.

This is where a lot of us....women, girls, ladies...get hung up! Where is the thin line between the girlfriend duties and the wife duties? I love to cook...so quite naturally I have always cooked for the men I have dated. But some older women would say that is something on his "wife" should be doing. I like a clean home. So....quite naturally...if I am spending a lot of time at my guy's home, I may do some cleaning. But again, is that only something that a "wife" should only be doing. In my most honest opinion, neither of these are specific to a girlfriend or wife...it is specific

Mrs. Nakisha S. James

to the maturity of the people involved. A good man will not take advantage of his girlfriend who cooks and cleans but will see those as good qualities for her becoming his wife. Just as a good woman won't stop cooking and cleaning, if that is who she is, just because she isn't married to the man she's with. If more people would truly be themselves and not let society dictate what should and should not take place in their households, then all these things become irrelevant in the relationship.

If you feel a certain way about something stand firm in your feelings. It's a reason why you have that feeling in the first place.

This one was a big one for me. I had to choose whether to go along with what seemed to be MR. RIGHT or stand firm in my belief and morals. This was not an easy thing to do. Especially when you want something so bad and you feel that God was the one who sent this person into your life. But I have learned that whatever or whoever GOD places in your life will be just right for your life. It will be crystal clear. Now I'm not saying that everything will be all peach cobbler and banana pudding but for the most part your life will be enhanced and not made complicated by this person. And being unequally yoked isn't something God would put on you.

Mrs. Nakisha S. James

to have something you've never had you must do something you never did.

If you have never skydived how will you ever know the adrenalin rush of sky diving unless you what....?? Go Skydiving! Just like, how will you ever know what the outcome of any situation will be unless you go forth into that situation. I could've not called Mr. Chestnut and said oh well, he lost my number, so I am going to conveniently lose his. But if I had done that then I would have lost a big piece of my life that was meant to happen. I would not have my beautiful daughters that I have. I would not have been taught the lessons I was about to learn over the next 10 years of marriage. Yeah...big lessons for sure! Keep Reading...

Mrs. Nakisha S. James

CHAPTER 6

Marriage Mayhem

FIRST COMES LOVE...OR LUST

The very next week after Mr. Morris and I begin dating unfortunately his father passed. We had had many conversations about his dad and what a man he was. He was very ill and was living in a nursing home at the time. Mr. Morris would always go visit his dad often in the home. We had even talked about me going with him to visit. But as fate would have it his dad got tired and gained his wings. I remember I was at work at my desk when I got the call. My heart sank into my stomach. I knew how much he loved his dad. I had some time off I could take so I left work to go be with him to comfort him at this awful time. As the week progressed, arrangements were made for his father. He was a deacon at their family church. When the day came for the funeral, I was asked by Mr. Morris to attend. So of course, I did. That morning I get dressed and I head out to the South Side of the city where

Mrs. Nakisha S. James

the church was located. I arrive to the church and there were cars everywhere! This man was very well known if by looking at the number of cars were present. I walk in and I look for Mr. Morris. He was asked by his dad before his death that he would preach his eulogy. When I looked, I saw him sitting at the front in the pulpit of the church. I went to grab me a seat in the back of the church. When the service was over, the funeral home reopened the casket so friends and family can one more time go around to say their goodbye's. Now anyone who knows me knows that I am terrified of funerals and dead people. If I really do not have to attend a funeral I WON'T! So, for me to be at this funeral where I know absolutely no one there, not even the deceased, was a big stretch for me! When they reopened the casket, for support of Mr. Morris I walked around to view the body. Lord please give me the strength! Mr. Morris was standing there next to his father's remains. When I walked up there...I looked at his dad and then I looked at him....splitting image!! It was like I was looking at an older version of Mr. Morris laying there in that box! That really spooked me! I moved on and I gave Mr. Morris a hug. I remember it was extra tight and I kind of made him smile. But Lord when I turned around to walk back to my seat the looks that I got from the women in that church. If looks could kill, they would have laid me right next to his dad! Afterwards at the repass, Mr. Morris and I were sitting eating and there were people coming over to hug him and give their condolences. Some of the women introduced themselves to me and were very friendly but there were others that had this look of disguise as to why am I with "their" man. I just laughed. He never introduced me as his girlfriend or anything but **when your light shines so bright no introduction is needed.** I met all the brothers and sisters...8 sisters and 7 brothers. That was overwhelming to say the least! I will never forget, after everything was over and some time had passed, Mr. Morris said to

Mrs. Nakisha S. James

me "My dad held on to life for me. He wanted to make sure I was okay. When I went to see him that last week and I told him about you, I guess he knew I was going to be okay and he let go. God never takes something away from you unless he plans to bless you with something/someone equal or better." Wow! That blew me away! In that moment I begin to think about my mom and how God blessed me with my Momma She-She not even a year after she passed. Momma She-She without a doubt was placed in my life by nobody but God. He knows who and what we need at the exact time we need them!

Time went on and me and Mr. Morris' relationship grew stronger. He left the southside of the city and moved way out to Carol Stream where I was. One day we were home just sitting around watching television and he asked if I would please get him a glass of water. I go to the kitchen, grab a glass out of the cabinet, and proceed with getting his water out of the faucet. (This was when it was safe to drink faucet water) He says, "No I want it colder." I go into the fridge to get the water I had in a pitcher. He says, "No No I want ice." So of course, if you know me, by this time I'm about ready to tell him he too damn picky and come in here and get your own damn water!! But I open the freezer to get the ice and there was a surprise in there. A Kay's ring box and a note that said, "Will You Marry Me?" OMG! I open the box and it was the exact ring I had told him I wanted. WOW! Lord you really showing out this time!! He came in the kitchen and put the ring on my finger and waited for my answer. YES!!!!! OF COURSE, YESSSS!!! This is the day that I had been waiting on for years! And finally, it had come true! But there was one thing...he had not talked to my dad. Even though my dad and I were not on the best of terms most of the time I still respected him as my father and if any man wanted to marry me, they had to

Mrs. Nakisha S. James

ask my dad's permission. Some days past and he finally gathered the nerve to ask. I was not on the phone when they talked so I can not say exactly what took place during that conversation. But the wedding planning began immediately.

What colors should we have? How man bridesmaids and groomsmen do we need? Who will be the maid of honor and the best man? Where will we get the cake? Decisions, Decisions! But the biggest decision would be WHERE!? We both agreed that we wanted to do a destination wedding. Somewhere on a nice beautiful beach with beautiful warm weather. Jamaica! Negril, Jamaica. We found a travel agent and begin planning everything. How exciting! ***But not everyone will always be excited about what you are excited about.**

Not too long after we this I stopped by to see my dad. I was telling my dad about the plans we had for Jamaica. My dad drilled me for 3 hours saying that would be selfish on my part to have my wedding so far away from so many friends and family that most likely could not afford to travel away. He said neither of my grandmothers would be able to go. My dad knew that it was important for me to have my loved ones there for this special event and anything that would prevent that I would not do. He mentioned how expensive it would be for people to travel to Jamaica. After this conversation with my Dad, I began to rethink some things and took the information back home to talk it over with my fiancée. He was not too thrilled about changing our plans, especially since we had already put money down and would lose our deposit but changed everything to have the wedding in IL. The wedding planning went from having 10 months to plan to now 6. That's not very much time to plan! But we did! Ten bridesmaids, 10 groomsmen, 2 best men, a maid

Mrs. Nakisha S. James

and a matron of honor, 2 flower girls, cake, DJ, delicious catering, reception hall and an outdoor ceremony in 80-degree weather. We had about 150 guest which was very nice. Everything came together beautifully with both my grandmothers in attendance. There were even a couple of surprises my wedding party had pulled off for us. And there were even more surprises to come! Keep Reading...(**Even though things may not be exactly the way you had originally planned that does not mean that things must turn out bad)**

THEN COMES BABY

---

*Now that the wedding was over it was time to be married. Back to life and back to reality. Now that all the flowers are gone, all the catered food has been eaten, all the guest have gone home, it was now time to be husband and wife. And what exactly did that mean? Were there certain roles we needed to adhere to? Does this mean I had to listen and DO everything this man asked of me? Is that what being submissive meant? We had counseling before we gotten married but there were still many unanswered questions. And things were about to get even more complicated.

I remember I was on Depo Provera birth control. The shot that you get in your butt every 3 months. (And I don't know how in the world I kept that up and I HATE needles)! I was told by my doctor that the injection can stay active in your body for several months even after you are no longer taking the shots. The new husband and I did want to have children eventually. We decided that I would stop getting the injection a few months after the wedding. To our surprise I got pregnant IMMEDIATELY. **Some doctors really do not know what in the world they are talking about!** It was March 2004 when I found out I was pregnant. My due date was December 11, 2004. We had just said our I Do's in July 2003 and now I'm already about to have my first child. This was so exciting but so unexpected!

Months past and here I was just getting bigger and bigger! Wow I was really going to have a baby. A little girl named Winter Jicole. I could not wait to meet her. I remember when I first felt her kick. It was on our first-year anniversary July 12, 2004. I never had any morning sickness or swelling or any of the things that most pregnant women have. You really couldn't even tell I was pregnant unless I turned around and you saw my belly. The 9 months I spent carrying my first baby was so wonderful. I remember on December 4, 2004 I went into labor at 7am. I was home and the husband had just left for work. I remember feeling some pains in my back and my stomach but I didn't believe it was labor. I called my husband to tell him I may be in labor. He did a 360 and turned right back around to rush back home. Luckily, my brother-in-law was home and took me to the hospital. The entire ride to the hospital all my bro-n-law kept saying was "Please don't have the baby in my car!" And he was dead serious. I promise this man drove 90mph the whole way to the hospital. Scared me half to death! My husband met us there. After some hours of being in Triage the doctor said I had not dilated enough and the contractions were not close enough to keep me there. They couldn't keep me. So back to my home I went with my labor pains. They were close enough for me!! I don't know what they were talking about! While at home I was in labor for 12+hours!! I walked up the stairs and down the stairs. I walked through the kitchen and back to the living room.

Mrs. Nakisha S. James

I walked all around my home I swear it felt like 1000 times or more! LORD HELP ME!! I knew after 12 hours of all that I HAD to have dilated some more. My Aunt Rene and cousin LaShauna were there at my home to help keep me motivated to keep moving around as much as I could. Finally, around 9pm that evening I had had enough. "TAKE ME BACK TO THE HOSPITAL BECAUSE THIS BABY IS COMING OUT TODAY!" Back to Mercy Medical Center I went. After 25 ½ total hours of excruciating labor pains, my beautiful baby girl had arrived. 7lbs 7oz beautiful baby girl. This baby had dimples so deep in her little face even all the nurses were at awe! I cried when I first saw her smile. The nurse asked me what was wrong, why was I crying. I told her that I could not believe GOD loved me so much to bless me with such a beautiful little girl! The tears just kept rolling down my face. What a true blessing. And she still is a blessing now 15 years later.

NO MORE GREENS AND CORNBREAD

After the birth of Winter, I knew that I had the perfect marriage, the perfect life. I had my husband who was preaching in churches across the Chicagoland area, I had my beautiful doll face daughter, everything was perfect. So, I thought. Things started to fall apart. My husband got injured at work and had to file for workman's compensation. He was given the run around so much with this process. So, he wasn't receiving any income. This took place for months! I was home with Winter and wasn't working at the time. I did find work eventually and we kind of got back on track. At the time during my last few months of pregnancy we were living with

Mrs. Nakisha S. James

my brother-in-law. When I started working, we were able to get approved to rent a Townhome out in Aurora, IL. It was a beautiful 2 story townhome, 2 car garage, nice backyard, just the place to raise a family. It was a rent to own property. We signed a 12-month lease with the hopes of purchase after the 12 months were done. As luck would have it, the contract I was under at my job ended right before the 12 months ended. When the owner came to us about buying the property, we were not able to at the time. We had to vacate our home. Between this time and throughout the next 7 years we had moved a good 7 or 8 times. We moved pretty much every year. Him in and out of work and me end and out of contracts nothing seemed to be stable. *But we had each other and each other's back through thick and thin. The way a marriage should be. It was us against the world. Through thick and thin, the good and the bad, no matter what. I guess THIS was what marriage was all about. About 3 years after Winter was born, I found out I was pregnant with our second child. Another baby girl was on the way. We named her Serenity J'Vonni. She didn't look real when she was born. She looked like a baby doll with a TON of hair on her head! The husband really wanted a boy but another girl was fine with me. During this time, we were living in Hammond, IN. We were able to get approved for an apartment there. Yes, there was a lot of moving even across state lines. Things still seemed to be going fine. That was the perception. Behind my back there were some extracurricular activities going on. It seems as if I wasn't the only woman my husband seemed to be interested in. There were a few text messages and some inappropriate conversations that were had with some so called "friends" of his. And yes, I was still pregnant at the time with our second daughter. Serenity would be her name. She was born November of 2007. Once again GOD had blessed us with a gorgeous doll face child. Unbelievable! We were still living in Hammond at the time.

Mrs. Nakisha S. James

It wasn't the best place to live but not the worst. Some new neighbors had moved into the apartment next door. When the moved in they brought some little critters with them. YES ROACHES!!! Now ANYBODY who TRULY knows me KNOWS I am deathly terrified of bugs! My motto has been and will always be "If you have more legs than me you can't stay in my home!" I saw one little critter in my kitchen I said okay let me call the office to tell them they need to come and spray. Then I saw another in my bathroom...I said, "AW HELL TO THE NO HONEY!" I immediately called down to the management office to tell them about this issue. The management company came and had my place exterminated but that did nothing! Even the management office told us that the people that moved in next door was not on the "clean" side and we would continue to get "critters" from their apartment no matter how many times they came to spray. So, if they knew they were not on the "clean" side then why would you let them move into your property? That told me all I needed to know about the place! So, guess what....we had to move again! God please be some stability! We were in the middle of our 12-month lease but I was not going to stay anywhere that I did not feel comfortable and my babies were not safe! There would be no bugs crawling in any ears in here!!! No sir! We moved again and broke that lease! And because we had broken our lease there at the apartment in Hammond, no other apartments would approve us. We were essentially homeless with 2 babies. I called my Auntie Nae Nae. I explained to her our situation. All she had was her concrete basement to offer. Well it was better than being out in the cold. I appreciated her for opening her home to us. We began to move our items into her basement. I tried to make it a home as best I can for my babies. I recall a day Winter was coming down the stairs from the kitchen. She was only 3 years old. The stairs leading to the basement didn't have any sides on them. There was only the wooden

Mrs. Nakisha S. James

68

steps and the banisters on each side. Winter being only 3 and short her arms could not reach the banisters to hold on to as she walked down the stairs. I'm sitting on the bed changing Serenity's diaper when I glance over and I see Winter slowly falling off the stairs under the banister. Remember I said earlier my Aunt's basement was all CONCRETE! I quickly go over to where she was. She had fallen behind an old desk that was down by the stairs. I looked at her laying there on her side. She wasn't moving. I immediately ick her up and I see this long gash on the side of her head from her eyebrow all the way to her ear. My baby was bleeding and not moving. It seemed like an eternity but a few seconds later she began to cry. Oh my God I was a nervous wreck! Then Serenity began to cry because I left her on the bed all alone. I took Winter over to the sink and grabbed a towel to wash off her face. Tears started to roll down my face. What kind of Mother am I to have my children living under these conditions? I felt horrible. The husband wasn't there. When I got Winter all cleaned up, and both girls settled, I called him. "WE HAVE TO GO!!" I said. He asked, "What's the problem?" I begin to explain to him what happened with Winter and how staying here in this concrete basement was not going to work. I loved my Aunt and appreciated her so much but after that incident I just couldn't imagine what else could happen. A few days had passed and it was time to go. I had to go for my sanity. We could not get approved for any apartment so we ended up residing in an extended stay hotel over in Villa Park, IL. This is a Western Suburb of Chicago. I had just given birth to my second baby girl and now I was homeless living in a hotel. What else could happen now God?... Keep Reading...

A good friend of mine....we will call her "Ms. B" had offered my family to move in with her. Her and her husband had a huge home and had enough room for

Mrs. Nakisha S. James

myself, my husband and our two little girls. I had confided in her and was telling her about our situation. I needed some type of outlet to get all this stuff off my mind. When I brought it to my Mr. Husband he declined. So, there we were in this hotel with our 2 children. Some months passed and my friend would steadily be offering her home to us. So, I had had enough and I moved with her. Yes, I left the hotel and I took our two daughters with me. We were barely making our payments every week there and the hotel was not the placed I wanted to raise my girls. Mr. Husband was so mad when I left and he felt that I no longer stuck to the "for better or for worse" part of our marriage. And I truly did understand his reasoning but I also had 2 children that needed to be somewhere besides in a hotel. He couldn't see that. He also ended up leaving the hotel and moving in with the same brother where we were living with just a few years earlier. (Now remember when I said my husband was "entertaining" some other women besides his wife....keep reading....)

Living with "Ms. B" was bittersweet. I was happy to be out of that hotel but I did miss my husband and our family being together. Winter would ask all the time where her Daddy was and why we were not together. It's kind of hard to explain to a 4-year-old why her parents are not under the same roof. I considered "Ms. B" to be my closest friend at the time. I mean after all I was living under her and her husband's roof. Her husband was also a preacher like mine. So that kind of gave me a little comfort while living there. I thought my girls and I were safe. I thought that she had my back. Whenever my husband I would have a disagreement or if I felt alone and afraid about the shambles of life, I would confide in her. ***I learned very quickly that even the people that are in the same home with you can be against you.**

Mrs. Nakisha S. James

70

It was July 12, 2008. (I remember this date specifically because it was our 5th year wedding anniversary) It was poring down raining outside. I was awakened out of my sleep by my friend, "Ms. B's" husband. It was about 2am. He asked in a very concerned tone "What is your husband's cell number?" I told him. He had his wife's phone. He showed it to me. I see my husband's phone number saved in her phone as "Poppy" Poppy?!?!?! What the hell?! He goes on to show me a whole book load of text messages between his wife and "Poppy". Then he goes into her voicemail and I hear voicemails "Poppy" had left on her phone. Shocked isn't even the term I would use for the feeling I had at that moment. Utter disappointment, betrayal, Anger......RAGE is more like it!!! My babies were laying there sleeping so peacefully and I'm up trying not to go downstairs and stab this bitch to death! I don't know how he, her husband, managed not to slap her in her sleep. So, what did I do next? Well what any other high-class woman would do. I got up, got myself dressed, I began packing my shit, I dropped my babies to my dad's, and I waited....FOR HOURS....for my husband to come over. Remember I said it was our 5th year anniversary so he was coming by anyway. Winter was sick the night before. I told him if her fever had not gotten better, I was going to take her to the ER. So, I texted him early and told him she had not gotten better and that I needed him to come over ASAP!!! You know....so we can take her to the ER together. (Winter was just fine by the way) Meanwhile, "Ms. B's" husband was doing everything under the sun to stay away from his wife because he didn't want to choke the hell out of her. He was outside sweeping the sidewalk. He would go in the basement. Just anything to stay away from her. I was sitting on the couch waiting for my husband to arrive at the house. "Ms. B" had the audacity to come and sit with me and ask me "So what

Mrs. Nakisha S. James

are you and your husband doing today for your anniversary?" Now wait a damn minute....did she just sit right in my face and ask me that?! After the voicemails that I heard between her and Mr. Husband...did she just ask me that?!! This broad had some pretty big kahunas! I just smiled and said "I don't know. We will just have to see what happens when he gets here." Her husband and I had already put together our plan once "Poppy" arrived. He was going to whoop his ass and I was going to tear a new hole in hers!

Finally, he pulls up. He gets out the car and walks up to the house. The door is open so I could see him through the screen door the whole time. I could also see "Ms. B's" husband walking closely behind him. (Remember I said he was out sweeping the sidewalk just to stay away from his wife) They both come in the door. My husband says, "What's up?" I respond, "Oh I don't know POPPY! Why don't YOU tell me WHAT'S UP!?" he looks confused. I turn to her and I said, "So who is POPPY?" The look of shock quickly took over her face. She began to say something but before I knew it, I had lunged her way hands straight out aiming for her neck! My husband grabbed me from behind to prevent my hands from reaching her face. Her husband went over and grabbed her and they began to argue. I had already packed all of me and my girl's things and put them in my truck! I was ready to whoop ass and never to return to her home ever again. I walked out the door to get in my truck, my husband followed close behind me. He got in the passenger side. "Kisha I'm so sorry, please forgive me, I'm sorry." All I wanted to know was why?? Why her? The friend that you said you didn't trust. We are all the way here in the West Suburbs, you were all the way on the South Side of Chicago and yet you want to cheat with not only my closest friend but the woman I am currently residing with. I

Mrs. Nakisha S. James

72

just don't understand it. I found out they had met up at the very hotel that he and I spent our wedding night. Talk about no respect! ***Sometimes when a man says he does not "trust" your friend and he doesn't want YOU around her...that may be for his own benefit.**

JUST TIRED

Being betrayed by my closest friend and my husband took a tremendous toll on me. I really believe I had a nervous breakdown. I ended up going to my dad's and staying with him and his wife. Down the street from my dad's home was a park. I would go down there almost daily and cry my eyes out. My girls never knew anything. No matter what I never showed them I was sad or hurt. I always made sure to keep a smile on my face when I was with my girls. ***But kids are not dumb.** Winter would ask me all the time "Mommy what's the matter? I feel like you are sad." She was so observant. But of course, I did not tell her of what had happened. I mean she was only 4 years old. How would I explain all this to her?

Time moved on and I gotten stronger. My dad's wife had pulled some strings and gotten me hired at Blue Cross and Blue Shield downtown. I did not want to leave my babies but I could not wait to start work and get back on my feet and into my own home. With all that had happened my children and I needed some stability and fast!! Luckily, I was told about a home daycare that Serenity could attend. Thank you Lord! I surely did not want to enroll her in one of those

Mrs. Nakisha S. James

"corporate" day care centers that cost you an arm and a leg! Serenity started attending Ms. Octavia's Home Daycare. It was perfect. Her home wasn't too far from where I could park and catch the Metra or the 'L' to work. She was so nice and loved all her babies! (Octavia and I are still good friends to this day. Love her to Life) So I began work, Winter was still at her preschool and I had Serenity going to the new home daycare. Things seem to be looking up. I began to look for an apartment for me and my girls to live. I appreciated and loved my dad and his wife for allowing us to stay with them during my time of devastation, but I really needed my own. I stumbled up on an apartment literally a few blocks from my dad. I called the number and talked to the owner. It was a private owned property so I didn't have to go through all the hassle with my credit and background. I gave the owner a brief run down of what I was going through and he understood. I signed the lease and moved in 30 days later. There is a GOD!! The apartment wasn't much to write home to Momma about. But it was mine and I was happy! *A peace of mind beats luxury any day! I didn't have any furniture or pots and pans. I didn't have a bed or bath towels. I really didn't have too much of anything but my clothes and my babies. But the joy I had was priceless! Eventually things came together. I had bought an air mattress for us to sleep on for the time being. My girls thought it was just a big balloon for them to play on. Everything was okay but not perfect. A month or so had passed and I began to get my home together. Before long Winter began to ask questions like "Can Daddy come and stay the night" and "Why doesn't Daddy live here with us?" Now what do you say to a 4-year-old who asked these questions? I would quickly try and change the subject every time she would ask. I never kept my girls away from their dad during this whole ordeal. He would call and talk to them and come by and see them. Our issue was not their problem. After a few months he and I began to have regular adult conversations. When I first left, I didn't have two words to say to him. But for the sake of our children and as an example for them I put my anger and disappointment to the side. Eventually he began to stay the night. Before long he had he moved in. ***The girls were so happy when we were all together and I didn't want to take that away from them.** Even though my trust was not 100% there with him (hall after that whole incident it wasn't even .1% there...but for my babies) I let him back in to my life. But I was in a 1-bedroom apartment with an air mattress. This was not going to work. I talked to the landlord and just so happened he had a 2 bedroom that was becoming available for rent in the next few months. When that apartment was open and available, we moved in. Luckily it was right upstairs from where we were. We purchased some furniture, put some artwork on the walls and called it home. My girls were happy. It seemed my husband was happy. Me on the other hand...keep reading

DASH TO DIVORCE

Finally, some stability had come into our lives. I was working at BCBS. My husband had gotten a job as the dean of students at a school in Chicago. Both girls were happy with having both their parents at home. The daycare Serenity was in was working perfectly! Winter was doing very well in preschool. I had even registered and gotten back in school to finish my degree. On top of going to school I had gotten involved in an MLM company called LegalShield. We went from neither of us being

Mrs. Nakisha S. James

employed just a few short years prior to us having multiple streams of income. All was going so well.

It was almost April and time for my 35th birthday. This birthday was so very special to me because at age 35 was when my mom gained her wings. I had planned this big celebration for myself and to honor my mom. But it wasn't going to be just any party. I decided to do a Mardi Gras themed party because one thing my mom enjoyed doing was going to Mardi Gras. I hired event planner extraordinaire Ms. Bri Bridges to help pull this off. And pulled it off she did!! We had all the colors of Mardi Gras the gold and purple and green. We had Mardi Gras mask and beads. We even had a fake streetlamp post that had Bourbon Street on it! I'm telling you this placed looked like Mardi Gras in New Orleans! It was amazing!!!! A few days before the big day my husband started to come down with a cold. We tried to knock it out with tea and some other medicines but nothing worked. The day of my party his was not feeling his best. I told him to stay home but he insisted that he go to the party. He sat in the corner most of the night. We were able to snag a few photos of him. When all the festivities were over, we headed straight home. When he woke up the next morning, he said he felt a little better. We decided to go have breakfast. Our girls were at his sister's house so we had time before we needed to pick them up. He hopped in the shower while I began to pick out my clothes for the day. His cell phone was sitting over on his nightstand. It buzzed. I thought nothing of it. Then it buzzed again...and again...and again...AND AGAIN! Okay so now everyone knows this is my birthday weekend so who is trying to get a hold of my husband at this time of morning....maybe it's bis sister and it's something with the girls.....no she would have called me if he could not reach him...okay so...buzz...buzz...buzz! I go look at his

Mrs. Nakisha S. James

phone and its text message after text message after text message from some woman....we will call her "Ms. Peoria." The messages were something like "HEY BOO...are you feeling better? I know you said that you were coming down with something a few days ago. I just wanted to check in on you. How was your wife's party that you threw for her? Was she grateful? Because if I were your wife, I would not have gone but I would have stayed home and took care of you. Call me when you can get free." What in the *#(@%(_#!! The party you threw for me?!!? If I was your wife?!?!? Was I grateful?!?!?!?! Mad...naw...Livid...nope...Complete Utter Rage to the 100th power of PISSTIVITY!! Are you FUCKING kidding me!? After all the BS we went through with "Ms. Brown" and I take you back you have the BALLS to do this shit again!!!!! Oh God is just going to have to forgive me and I am just going to have to repent for what I am about to do!!

He gets out the shower, looks at his phone, reads the text, TEXT BACK, and then ask me "Where do you want to go have breakfast?" WHAT THE WHAT?? "I'm not hungry." "Why aren't you hungry now?" he said. "I'm just not." I said. "Well you know I have to go up to the school and let the church in to have service (a local church didn't have a church building and they would have their services up at the gym at the school where he worked at. So, every Sunday he would go up there to let them in for their afternoon service) "Yes I know...go!" "Kisha what is wrong with you now??" I was so hurt and out done that I was really going through this crap again with him that I became numb and speechless. I couldn't talk, I just felt......empty. I thought about my girls and how this would affect them. I have a million thoughts running through my head and a million emotions running through the rest of my body. If I would have acted on my emotions at THAT time I for sure

Mrs. Nakisha S. James

would be locked up and on an episode of First 48. I said nothing. He left. I'm sure he called "Ms. Peoria" as soon as he got in the car. So now do I burn all of his Michael Jordan shoes first or do I bust a hole in this 70" TV! Nope...I won't do either. Again, I will take the high road and be an adult. My phone buzzes...it's him texting me. "Are you okay." "I will be" I responded. "You will be? So, what does that mean Kisha?" So, who is..."Ms. Peoria"?" I asked. "Who is who??" ..."Ms. Peoria" "I don't know who that is. Where did you get that name from?" he said "She texted you this morning wanting to check on you to make sure her BOO was okay since she knew you had been sick. Oh, and she wanted to know how my party was that you threw for me...." "Kisha listen....CLICK!!! I hung up. Buzz, buzz, buzz. Ring, Ring, Ring. Buzz. Ring. Ring. Buzz. I was so outdone. I was so hurt. I was so in shock AGAIN! He goes and gets our girls, and he comes home. I'm sure he was shocked to see the house still in one piece. I hugged and kissed my babies and I continued doing whatever I was doing. "Kisha can we talk." Ignore. "Kisha please can we talk" "Talk? I think you have been doing enough talking to "Ms. Peoria." You keep on doing that. I'm good!" I responded. "No Kisha see you got it wrong." All I heard was Blah Blah Blah....Lie, lie lie. I wasn't listening to shit he had to say! Hours passed and I tucked my babies in bed and then I got ready for bed. He came and got in the bed. I got up and went on the couch. He came and followed me onto the couch (We had a huge sectional) I went and got back in the bed. This happened every night for a few days and then he got the picture and he stayed on the couch. Two weeks had passed. This night he came and got in the bed. When I tried to get up, he grabbed me and held me and began to cry. I don't think I had ever seen him cry. He held me and he cried, and he said "Kisha I don't want to lose you again. I don't want to lose my family. Please listen to me. "Ms. Peoria" is a girl I knew back in 8th grade and we JUST became

Mrs. Nakisha S. James

friends on Facebook. (Remember this now April/May...this will be an important factor later) "Yes I told her I was sick and I told her about your party but we just started talking I swear! Please forgive me. She is married with 2 boys and lives all the way in Peoria, IL. I am not cheating on you with her. I promise!" He is now crying big crocodile tears. (I had never seen him cry like that...not even when his father passed away.) So of course, ole softy me, let him back in AGAIN! For better or for worse...for richer or for poorer...in sickness and in health.

A month or so passed. It was June to be exact. I was still in school at the time. On the weekend was when I had the most time to complete my homework. But again, on the weekend was when my husband had to go up to the school and prepare it for the church to meet there on Sunday. It was Saturday afternoon. He had to go up to the school...his job...to take care of some stuff before the church had services there the next day. Me and the girls went with him. The girls would go with him sometime and play in the gym while he worked. I decided to go this day. My laptop wasn't working at the time and so I asked if I could borrow his (the one his job gave him for work) so that I could submit my homework assignments. "Sure" he said. I go into one of the empty classrooms to have some privacy and quiet while he went and did what he needed to do. Our girls followed me. I sit at one of the desks and I open the laptop. I log in and I clicked onto Yahoo so that I could go into my account and submit my class work for school. Well, when I clicked on Yahoo his Inbox popped right up in front of me. And what's the first name I see.......""Ms. Peoria" Now, for those that know me know that I do not go and look for trouble because **when you go looking for trouble you will definitely find it.** However, if trouble pops

Mrs. Nakisha S. James

up right in front of your face, then it's your responsibility to handle it! That's my theory!

I click on the first email email...which had a very recent date attached...and not to my surprise the email talks about them getting together soon. It's funny...I was mad but not surprised. I continued to go down the list of emails with this familiar name attached. Would you know I found emails that dated way back to February?! But remember he said in APRIL, the day after my birthday, that they had JUST became friends on Facebook. Some of these emails talked about this lady coming to my home to spend some time there with my husband while I would be away on a business trip that was coming up soon. Emails with pictures attached!! (I'm going to let your imagination take you away with what type of pictures were shared!!) Emails about my daughters and how she could not wait to meet them! WTF!!! Here we go AGAIN!!!!!!!! Lord please give me patience because if you give me strength I'm going to jail!!!! And remember our daughters were right there in the room with me. Of course, going through all these emails, I didn't get any homework done. So, I did what any woman would do...I emailed "Ms. Peoria"...from my husband's Yahoo account. Did I mention this is the email account that I set up for him AND this was his laptop provided to him by his employer?! I don't believe sending photos of yourself to a woman that isn't your wife was part of the job description or part of the policy for the use of this laptop. After seeing all of this I sent a nice little email from his email address. Basically, stating that this is MRS. SIMMONS and your little rendezvous that you are having with MR. HUSBAND has been busted wide open. I asked her, "Does YOUR HUSBAND and YOUR CHILDREN know about the dirty little pictures you are sending to another woman's husband?"

Mrs. Nakisha S. James

Oh yes, I went in but I didn't use not a single curse word. ***See you can tear a person apart without cursing them out.** My husband was in another part of the school at this time. He had no clue what was happening! And what was ABOUT to happen! After I hit send on my little email, I kindly closed his laptop, gathered my children and I left him at the school. I kindly called him as I was driving away and explained what I discovered. I told him I was done and it was over! I am nobody's doormat! I tried to work on this thing for years but it takes two to make it work. He of course tried to deny everything, but the proof was right there. No more guessing about nothing anymore! I was so done and it was so over!!

He found a ride home. Both the screen door and the house door were locked! He was beating on the door. I ignored it for a while but I didn't want the neighbors to be involved and my girls to be afraid. I finally let him in so not to cause a scene. He tried to talk to me but I just kept walking away. I had absolutely nothing to say and I sure as hell did not want to hear nothing he had to say! I told him he had to leave!! Pack your shit and go or no one will find your body!! After a few days he moved out. But now all the bills were on me. He was responsible for paying the rent. I was late with the rent and I had to tell my landlord what was going on. He told me that I was in luck. The girl across the way in the building across the street was moving out of her 1 bedroom and if I wanted it then it was mine. It was about $200 less than the 2 bedroom we were currently in. YES, absolutely I will take it! I can afford that! My girls and I would be a little cramped but it was something I could afford. ***God always shows up just when you need HIM to.** A week or so had passed and the young lady moved out across the street. My landlord gave me the keys and I began to move my girls and my things....ONCE AGAIN....out of the apartment. It was

Mrs. Nakisha S. James

a cute little one bedroom with a small kitchen and living area. As we were moving a peace fell over me. I gave my girls the room and I slept on an air mattress....ONCE AGAIN... in the living room. We crammed all our clothes and shoes into the one-bedroom closet as best we could. I went and bought some rugs and some wall art and I called it home. My girls and I called it home.

It is now near Christmas and of course my girls have been asking questions about their dad. Can he come and stay with us for Christmas? Is he ever going to come back home? There were some very tough questions I had to figure out how to answer to now my then 7 and 4-year-old. It was a really tough transition from being married with children, to being a single mom. I saw my mom be a single mom, my aunt, and some other friends and I just did not want that life. Not for myself or for my children. I wanted to change that vicious circle and be that 2-parent household that was, and still is, so scarce in the Black Community. I had said to myself long before I was even married that once I did get married, and especially when I had children, that I would NEVER get a divorce. I think God understood in this case why a divorce was the answer for me. That next year on Aug 9, 2012 I walked into a court room as a Mrs. and walked out a Ms. I was again a single woman. A Single Woman with children that is. It felt like a grand piano had been lifted off my shoulders when the judge stamped them papers! "Dissolution of Marriage granted!" the judge said. I left out the court room smiling from ear to ear!! Mr. Husband did not show up. Oh well! I left the court room, went and got my girls, and we went home to our peaceful stress-free one-bedroom apartment. God is so Good!

Mrs. Nakisha S. James

What I Gained – Lesson 6

> *when your light shines so bright no introduction is needed.*

It's funny how this works. Many times, we want the recognition from others and we want to feel included. But when you have this aura about yourself, a certain glow, no introduction is needed. Everyone that is paying attention (even when it's none of their business) will KNOW who and who's you are.

> *But not everyone will always be excited about what you are excited about*

In life we always want our family, friends and loved ones to be excited for us and have our back in the decisions we make in life. In a perfect world this will be the case. But in reality, not everyone that you think should be happy for you and that will support you won't. What I learned is when you decide to do something (especially with your mate/spouse) DO IT!! No matter what anyone has to say about it. In the end it's YOU that will have to live with that decision. I regret not following my first mind and not going to Negril when that's what we planned. But the wedding was still beautiful, nonetheless.

Mrs. Nakisha S. James

(*Even though things may not be exactly the way you had originally planned that does not mean that things must turn out bad)

God is ALWAYS in control! I don't care how you plan it, how you think want it, what you think it should look like...God is going to have the last say. And 100 times out of 100 HIS say is better than what I/we say ANYDAY!! Even though I was really down about not being able to have a destination wedding, things really did turn out beautifully. I learned sometimes when things look like they aren't going my way, just take a breath and wait for God. Everything will be just fine when you do!

*Now that the wedding was over it was time to be married.

Exactly what does being married mean? You plan your wedding, you pick the colors, you choose your wedding party, you find a hall and DJ....you do all of these things and dish out all of this money but not one of them have anything to do with being a husband or being a wife. The real challenge comes after the wedding day. In this marriage I learned so much about myself and all the strength I had inside of me. No one tests your "Gangster" more than a man who thinks HE GOT YOU and you not going anywhere. But KEEP READING...

Mrs. Nakisha S. James

Some doctors really do not know what in the world they are talking about

I know that Physicians go to school for 100 years to learn and practice a certain area of medicine. And even with all the knowledge and skills they learn mistakes still can happen. In my situation, me being told I won't get pregnant right away, it didn't "hurt" me. It just took us by surprise when we found out. But in many circumstances a mistake by a doctor can turn out to be detrimental. After this I learned to always go with your inner instinct. If something in you is tugging at you and telling you something is/isn't right....LISTEN!

But we had each other and each other's back through thick and thin. The way a marriage should be

Through the good, the bad and the ugly a husband and wife supposed to stick together. Just like gorilla glue! No one or nobody should be able to penetrate that bond. No income, living under someone else's roof, AND a small baby at the time...that's enough to overwhelm any couple. But we made it through. I learned a lot about my strength during this time. And I gained a lot of patience. I prayed A LOT too!

Mrs. Nakisha S. James

> *I learned very quickly that even the people that are in the same home with you can be against you.*

Not everyone that's in your house is in your corner. Blood relatives or people who you thought were just as close as blood can instantly turn on you and disappoint you to no end! This situation I found myself in so took me by surprise. Here I am with a 3-year-old and an 8-month-old, homeless, no job, living under a 'friend's" roof who behind my back is cheating on her minister husband with MY MINSTER husband. I leaned too to never put people on a pedestal. Minister's, preachers, the POPE or whoever. They are people just like everyone else and can and will fall to temptation if the opportunity presents itself. In the end trust yourself first and keep your friends out of your marriage. Confide in the LORD...or your Life Coach (Me ☺)

> *Sometimes when a man says he does not "trust" your friend and doesn't want YOU around her...that may be for his own benefit

You do remember early in the chapter when I said, "he didn't want to move in with her because he didn't trust her as my friend?" I found out why! That would have really messed some things up. But they both found out that day that whatever you do in the dark shall surely come to the light. I must admit this hurt me to my core. After all this happened, I couldn't think straight. I didn't eat for days. I would drive to the park up the street from my Dad's house and I would just sit in the car for hours and cry. I asked God "What did I do to deserve this?" I thought my marriage

Mrs. Nakisha S. James

86

was surely over. But what I learned from this time in my life is you never know how strong you really are until you are put in hot water. And this water right here was ON FIRE!!

*But kids are not dumb

Sometimes we think our children aren't as intelligent or observant as they really are. Children are just little people. They have the same mind, emotions, feelings as anyone else. They may not be able to express in full detail what they are feeling but believe me those feelings exist. As I was going through this rough time in my life, my oldest daughter was only 4 at the time. But I promise you she acted as if she was 44. And she was looking out for her Mommy. She would always hug me or kiss me when she saw that I was sad. She was my little best friend at the time. This was the only somebody that I could trust. And many times, your children are the only people you can trust.

*A peace of mind beats luxury any day!

I learned that we don't need the 6 bed/6 bath, 4 car garage, swimming pool in the backyard house to be happy. Now please do not get me wrong. Those things I just listed above are on my dream board to have but those things won't directly make me happy. When I was going through this time in my life, I felt pretty bad and worthless. When I started working and then was able to get my own place/space, my

Mrs. Nakisha S. James

87

spirits were lifted. It didn't matter how many bedrooms, as long as it was affordable and clean for me and my girls. My peace of mind trumped all that! And that's exactly what I got the say we moved in. WHOOSAHH!

> *The girls were so happy when we were all together and I didn't want to take that away from them.*

I know, I know, I KNOW what you are saying to yourself...now how in the hell did he finagle his was back in. My children are my #1 priority. Period! When I saw how happy they were to have their dad back in the home with them my heart melted. My whole life revolved around those two little girls and I would do anything to make them happy. Even put all my feelings, emotions, and happiness aside just to see them smile.

> *when you go looking for trouble you will find it*

I have never been the girlfriend or the wife that went snooping in my significant other's phone or personal items. I am a firm believer that whatever he is doing behind my back, if it is meant for me to find out I will. And I did in this case. There were so many lessons I learned through this whole transition in my life. But the one major lesson I took away was don't ever stay with someone because of your children. I tried to do that, and in the end, it still didn't work out. The two people involved in the relationship must want it and work for it for it to work. It takes the effort of both

Mrs. Nakisha S. James

individuals. And when it's only one sided it never works. When I became a single mom, my children became my #1 priority. It was ow me and them against the world!

> *See you can tear a person apart without cursing them out.*

I've learned the best way to give a person a piece of your mind is to speak calmly and with intelligence. In this situation I'm sure "Ms. Peoria" knew I was pissed! But, if you read that email, I sent to her, it was so calm but also straight to the point. You don't always have to be vulgar. I am a firm believer that what is done in the dark shall come to light. Her husband found out about her shenanigans. And not from me! God don't play!

> *God always shows up just when you need HIM to*

I had been through just about enough at this point. I had turned all my cheeks for this man and I had nothing more to give. When that apartment became available, at the time I needed it, and right at the price I could afford, I knew that was nobody but the big guy upstairs moving on my behalf. I learned that even in times of despair and turmoil, if you keep your faith things will ALWAYS work out in your favor! This is a promise!

Mrs. Nakisha S. James

CHAPTER 7

S.M.G. (Single Mother Grind)

WORK, SCHOOL, KIDS...REPEAT

The one thing that I never wanted to happen in my life had come true. I was now a single mother. And with not 1 but 2 babies to care and provide for all on my own. I had to work to pay the bills, make sure I had food on the table, help them with homework, do hair, iron clothes, clean the house, and still try to breath through it all. I did not know how hard being a single mother was until I was given this position. But I also did not know how strong I was. ***I learned that God will allow things to happen in your life that HE knows you are built for.** Mr. Husband would still come and get the girls every weekend. We didn't talk much when he would come by to pick them up. He was really upset that I went through with the divorce. I'm sure he NEVER thought I would have filed because I did share with him early on, when we were dating, that divorce wasn't for me. Well I guess I lied. Just like he lied. I wanted to try and be cordial and even friends for the sake of our daughters. He

Mrs. Nakisha S. James

wasn't having it! But *I am not that parent to keep my child away from their Father. My girls loved their dad and, in the end, it would only hurt them if I did. That was not on my agenda.

I was still working at Blue Cross and Blue Shield at that time. Catching the Metra train (and sometimes the Blue Line) downtown to work on most days. I had to have the girls off to school/daycare and be down at the station to catch my train at a certain time or I would miss it and then be late for work. On those snowy cold days this was the worse!! I had to make sure the girls were warmly dressed, take food out the freezer to cook later that night, start the car to let it warm up....just all the little things you kind of take for granted that you would have help getting done when there were 2 parents in the home. But I have to say I absolutely loved just me and my girls and our hot cocoa and movie nights! Just me with my babies. I made do with what I had and left the rest to God to provide. And HE did.

MY BABIES, MY BUSINESS, MY WELLBEING..........IN THAT ORDER

Working for Corporate America is very demanding. You have a time to be in the office, a time to take lunch, a time you can pee, a time to leave to go home, a time you can take off for sickness or vacation.....they dictate all of your time. And your time is the only one thing you cannot get back once it is gone. Now that it was

Mrs. Nakisha S. James

only me in the home, I needed more of my time to be dictated by me. Kids get sick, schools are closed for teacher conferences, stuff just happens where people, especially parents just need to have their time. When we were married Mr. Husband would pick up the kids every day from school and daycare. But now that we were no longer bound in holy matrimony, he didn't pick them up anymore. So that fell back on me. Many days this did not coincide with the time I finished at work. I had gotten written up so many times for leaving early and I was always in my managers office. Finally, one day she told me that she could no longer keep helping me and letting me get off with just a write up. The next time I was late coming in or left early then I would be terminated. WOW! This was my job, my income, my way of living! I could not lose my job. I went home that day and I really did some soul searching. A few years before my divorce I was introduced to a company called LegalShield that allowed me to make a living while working from home. I had only been doing it part time and at that time I really liked it. I loved the service and all that came with being an associate. I could make my own hours and then I could be available to be home when the girls got sick and I could pick them up from school without needing anyone's permission. That was so powerful to me. I prayed about it. I consulted with another single mother who was full time and doing very well in the business. I discussed my fears about me leaving my Corporate America job that pays me every two weeks to jump into something full time that would only pay me when I made a sale. I was terrified! The words that she said to me back then STILL resonates with me today. She said "You are a mother first before anything. You already know what is best for you to do." The next morning, I went into BCBS and I quit! I began doing LegalShield full time from that point on. No more of my time will be dictated by

Mrs. Nakisha S. James

anyone! PERIOD!! I've never looked back! ***Sometimes, even in fear, you must step out of your comfort zone and step into your faith!**

I dove right in headfirst into my business! Showing up to all the events, doing the personal development reading, making the phone calls, setting appointments...I was ALL IN. So much so that I was given the name "Fireball." That became my name throughout the team. While working in the business a young man caught my eye. We had worked together in the business before but now things looked different. I mean I am single now so.... We will call him "Mr. Two-Thirds." He was one of the Executive Directors in the company. We were great friends and so I felt I could share with him all that I had went through over the last year. He would come by with groceries and flowers and to check on me and the girls. It was nice to have someone very business minded and positive to spend time with. Nothing serious developed. ***I think I was an outlet for him as he was male comfort for me.** which in hindsight I was fine with that. I continued to move up the ladder in the business and make great strides. I began to train in front of the room and speak at many of the business briefings. Things were going very well. I was home with my babies when they needed me, I was making PTO meetings and anything else that my girls had going on I was there. This is every mother's dream. And I was living it. God is good!! But things were about to change dramatically AGAIN. Keep reading...

Mrs. Nakisha S. James

VENGEANCE IS MINE!

I was doing great in my business. I was getting paid everyday. I was meeting new people. I was being recognized and appreciated in front of many. It was so unlike my life in corporate America. I was so looking forward to going to the LegalShield International Convention in Las Vegas that year. Not only was it the convention but it was also my birthday weekend! YYAAYY! I could get some great life and business training and get lose for my birthday all at the same time! It was about 2 weeks before my trip. Tickets had been purchased and I was set to go. The girls would be on Spring Break. This was also at the same time their dad would also be off from work. PERFECT. We had already had this arranged for the girls to stay with him while I was gone. Suddenly, I get a text message from him that read... "How much am I going to get paid to watch the girls?" "Excuse me!?" I replied. He goes on to say..."Well if you were going to get a babysitter to watch them then you would pay them so how much are you going to pay me?" I was completely outdone! I'm like I got to be on an episode of PUNKD right now...where's the cameras? There is no way that a man that claims to love his children is asking to be paid to spend time with them. I got to be floating through the Twilight Zone! But he was serious! So serious that he told my daughters, who were so excited to be spending their Spring Break with their dad, that he could no longer watch them because I would not pay him. My baby came to me in tears begging saying "Mommy please pay Daddy so we can stay with him for Spring Break." Now it is one thing to mess with me but it's a whole different animal when you mess with my children! I am Momma bear protecting her cubs at all cost and against ANYBODY!! And guess what...he did not get his children.

Mrs. Nakisha S. James

With only 2 weeks left before I was to leave, I had to find a sitter. I was in luck. One of my mentors in the business had a 19-year-old daughter who the girls have been around numerous times and they absolutely loved her! She was very responsible, she drove her own car, and loved my girls as well. She was free and agreed to stay at my home and look after my girls while I was gone for the few days. Thank you Jesus! I felt secure with having her watch them. She was awesome!

I leave for my trip. I get to Vegas safely and I'm having a great time from the start! The whole time I was there my phone never stopped ringing. Mr. Husband was calling and texting trying to find his daughters. I did not answer. Not one call and not one text message. If he had kept with the agreement to keep his own children as he promised then he would know exactly where his daughters were! As long as I knew they were safe that was all that mattered! A few days had passed and my trip had come to an end. I came back home with a ship load of great information and I was a year older. But believe it or not, the actual night of my birthday I fell asleep and didn't not wake up until the next morning. So much for celebrating my new year of life. Nonetheless I had an awesome time. When I returned home my girls and their sitter had made me some very special gifts for my birthday. I was so grateful.

Maybe a week or two after I had returned from Vegas a knock came to my door. The girls were at school at the time and I was home making calls. I go to answer the door. "Who is it?" A voice says "It's _____ with DCFS." DCFS?! I open the door. There were two women with DCFS badges around their neck standing on my porch. "May we come in?" one of them said. "Sure" I said. They both came in

Mrs. Nakisha S. James

95

and sat down. "Would you like some water?" I offered. "No thank you." They both said. Pointing to the pictures all over my home one of the ladies asked, "Are these your 2 daughters?" "Yes ma'am" I responded. Then she began to tell me the reason for the visit. "We received a call about you leaving your daughters home without an adult while you went out of town for a week. Is this true?" WTH?! "This is considered a form of child neglect and we take these cases very seriously." "CHILD NEGLECT?!?! To who's child because not mine!?" I responded. "I would NEVER leave my children home alone without the proper supervision." She began to look around my home, saw more photos, saw some drawings the girls did that I attached to the fridge..."You love your children obviously." YES I DO VERY MUCH!" I replied. "Now where did these allegations come from about some child neglect!?" I asked. She said she could not give me the person's name but the report stated that I had left and went out of town for several days and I left my children in the care of a 15-year-old alone. ARE YOU FREAKING KIDDING ME?!?!? She asked if I had been out of town lately? "Yes" I said. "Did your children go with you?" she asked. "No they didn't" I replied. " Do you mind if I ask where they were while you were gone?" she asked. "They were right here in their own home with their 19-year-old sitter." I go on to tell her the whole story about their dad and all that happened in the previous week. I even showed her the text message of him asking to be paid to keep his own children! She says, "Well if you think about that story that you just told me then you probably can figure out who called us." "Yes I have an idea!" I said. I mean after all of the bullshit this asshole has already put me and my girls through NOW THIS!! "Your home is very warm and loving. I see nothing that shouts neglect here. Even your whole demeanor is calm. Usually, when we knock on someone's door and announce we are from DCMS they are so nervous and start sweating bullets. You are the total

Mrs. Nakisha S. James

opposite." She said. "That's because I have nothing to hide! I love my babies with everything in me and you can ask anybody who knows me! They will tell you!" I responded. The ladies completed their investigation at my home and left. My blood was boiling! Of all the things anyone can do to me or say about me, being neglectful to my children is the last freaking straw!! A few days later I had to take my girls up to her office so that they could question them. She said that she didn't see any signs of neglect at my home but she had to follow proper protocol to close the case. So, a few weeks later I took my babies up office. They were so cute with their hair all braided with beads. As they always are. When we got up to her office and she saw them her mouth dropped! "How beautiful are you two!!" She said. They just smiled. Winter showing her dimples and Serenity swinging her hair. She went ahead and started with the questions. I sat right there as she drilled my girls with a number of questions. "Do you believe your mommy loves you very much?" "Yes." They both answered. "Do you all eat every day?" "Yes." They both answered.' "Did your Mommy go out of town recently?" "Yes." They both responded. "Did your mom take you with her?" "No." they both responded. "And so who did you all stay with while your mom was gone?" She could not believe how detailed my daughters answered the questions and with honesty. After she finished with the girls, she came over to me and gave me a hug. She said "DCFS get so many false accusations everyday! Hundreds of calls of people who are mad at someone and so they think a great way to get back at them is to try and get their children taken away from them. It's such a shame. But you Ms. Simmons, you are so far from a neglectful parent! I have seen so many bad cases and yours is on the total opposite end of the stick. Your girls are adorable and very outspoken. Coming to your home and now meeting your daughters shows me this claim against you was absolutely false! There is no way I

Mrs. Nakisha S. James

believe you have ever been neglectful to your children!" All I could say was...Thank you GOD! She also told me because this was a false claim and we both knew who called it in that I could have that person prosecuted. "Oh REALLY!?" I said. The devil in me could not wait to get down to the police station!!! But *the God in me took over and said... "Just wait...I got something even better in store. Vengeance is mine!" Two months later myself and my two babies were on a plane relocating to sunny Arizona! HA! Deuces!

Mrs. Nakisha S. James

What I Gained – Lesson 7

I learned that God will allow things to happen in your life that He knows you are built for.

I never wanted to be a single Mother. I saw how my Mom struggled. I saw my aunt struggle. I just did not want to go through the same things they did. I vowed to myself that once I was married and had kids that I would never get a divorce. Never say never. God knew that my first husband and I were meant to be together only to bring 2 beautiful girls into this world. Our DNA had to come together for Winter and Serenity to be as beautiful as they are. And according to the good book it says that you should be married when are fruitful and multiply. So after we divorced, I understood it better and I knew that God had everything planned from the beginning. HE always does. And I knew that even though I had vowed never to get a divorce, after all that I had endured in this marriage, God said enough is enough my child. And I was set free.

Mrs. Nakisha S. James

> *I am not that parent to keep my child away from their Father. My girls loved their dad and, in the end, it would only hurt them if I did.*

I never have and I will never understand why any mother would keep their child(ren) from their father. Now if the father is abusive and toxic for the children then yes absolutely! But there are so many good dads out here that are hurting because they want to be apart of their child's life but the mom is in the way. Ladies please stop this! You are hurting your child. Even with everything that my girl's dad put me through and all that I had to endure I never once spoke bad about him to his children or kept them away from seeing him. As the kids get older, and if the dad is truly a deadbeat, the child(ren) will see it for themselves. There won't be anything that you will need to do. Believe me!

> *Sometimes, even in fear, you have to have step out of your comfort zone and step into your faith!*

When I said goodbye to my "good Corporate America" job I was terrified! It wasn't just me...I had to little people to take care of. Needless to say this LegalShield thing HAD TO WORK!!! And it did for that time on m life. Not only for income for me and my girls but also as legal help with all of these shenanigans I kept finding myself faced with. I still have the membership today. Better to have it and not need it than need it and not have it.

Mrs. Nakisha S. James

I think I was an outlet for him as he was male comfort

This guy and I had been working together in business for a few years. I saw he was somewhat of a lady's man. LOL! He will disagree with me. But at the end of the day he was a great friend and was there when I needed him the most. I was going through hell at this time in my life and to have someone come over to check on me and the babies was priceless. I learned through all of this that as a responsible SINGLE adult woman, it was okay to let my guard just a little to enjoy some male company. But my heart was still very much protected as you can imagine.

the God in me took over and said... "Just wait...I got something even better in store. Vengeance is mine!"

Even when it is prime time to repay someone for the wrong, they have done to you, sometime if you just take a breath, pray, and leave it in God's hands, HE will ALWAYS do you one better. I had always wanted to leave IL. I wanted to move right after my divorce. But my girls were still little at that time and I didn't want to take them away from all of their family and friends so soon. Plus, I had not heard from God to move just yet. And thank God I listened! Within 2 months after this I was doing quite well in my business and I also had been offered a work from home position in AZ! Life could not have been any better. But it did get much Much, MUCH better. But you have to get my next book to find out what I'm talking about. Smooches!

Mrs. Nakisha S. James

Letter to the Reader

Thank you again for going on this journey with me back through my life. Writing this book has been very liberating to say the least. It has been my therapy to come to grips with a lot that has happened in my short 43 years of life. (Yes, I'm 43...I look good for my age, don't I? HAHA!) This book was not meant to degrade or ostracize anyone. This book was written as a personal development book in hopes that whoever picks it up and reads it will know that they can conquer anything that life throws at them. And as you have read, in my life, I was thrown some pretty big stones. But I'm still here...I'm still standing. Thank you so much for your purchase and I hope that reading this will help you GAIN FROM YOUR PAIN. Love ya!!

Look out for my next book "What I Gained AFTER My Pain." Oh what a joy I have discovered after the drama. Stay tuned!!

Mrs. Nakisha S. James

Made in the USA
Las Vegas, NV
15 April 2021